Oracle® DBA
Guide to
Data Warehousing
and
Star Schemas

THE PRENTICE HALL PTR ORACLE SERIES
The Independent Voice on Oracle

Oracle® DBA
Guide to
Data Warehousing
and
Star Schemas

Bert Scalzo

PRENTICE
HALL
PTR
PRENTICE HALL
Professional Technical Reference
Upper Saddle River, New Jersey 07458
www.phptr.com

Library of Congress Cataloging-in-Publication Data

Scalzo, Bert
    Oracle DBA guide to data warehouse and star schemas : successful star schemas for
Oracle data warehouse / by Bert Scalzo.
        p. cm.
    Includes index.
    ISBN 0-13-032584-8
    1. Oracle (Computer file) 2. Data warehousing. I. Title

    QA76.9.D37S23 2003
    005.75'85--dc21   2003048817

Editorial/production supervision: *Donna Cullen-Dolce*
Cover design director: *Jerry Votta*
Cover design: *Nina Scuderi*
Art director: *Gail Cocker-Bogusz*
Interior design and composition: *Daly Graphics*
Manufacturing manager: *Alexis Heydt-Long*
Publisher: *Jeff Pepper*
Editorial assistant: *Linda Ramagnano*
Marketing manager: *Debby vanDijk*

© 2003 by Pearson Education, Inc.
Publishing as Prentice Hall Professional Technical Reference
Upper Saddle River, New Jersey 07458

Prentice Hall books are widely used by corporations and government agencies for training, marketing, and resale.

For information regarding corporate and government bulk discounts please contact:
Corporate and Government Sales (800) 382-3419 or corpsales@pearsontechgroup.com

Printed in the United States of America

10   9   8   7   6   5   4   3   2

ISBN 0-13-032584-8

Pearson Education LTD.
Pearson Education Australia PTY, Limited
Pearson Education Singapore, Pte. Ltd.
Pearson Education North Asia Ltd.
Pearson Education Canada, Ltd.
Pearson Educación de Mexico, S.A. de C.V.
Pearson Education—Japan
Pearson Education Malaysia, Pte. Ltd.

To my best friend in the whole world,
Ziggy,
my miniature schnauzer.

Contents

5 Tuning Ad-Hoc Queries   85

6 Loading the Warehouse   113

7 Implementing Aggregates   147

8 Partitioning for Manageability   169

9 Operational Issues and More   189

Index   205

Acknowledgments

I'd like to thank all the various employers and customers for whom I've had the pleasure of working on their data warehousing projects, most notably Citicorp, Tele-Check, Electronic Data Systems (EDS), and 7-Eleven. I'd also like to thank the numerous people in data warehousing that I've either met and/or learned from, including Ralph Kimball and Gary Dodge. I also owe much to the other DBAs with whom I've worked on data warehousing projects, including Ted Chiang, Keith Carmichael, Terry Porter, and Gerald Townsend. Finally, I owe a lot to Paul Whitworth, the best data warehousing project manager I ever worked for. Paul, more than anyone else, permitted me the time and freedom to develop into an expert on data warehousing.

Additionally, I offer special thanks to all the people at Prentice Hall for bearing with my busy schedule and special needs for time off while writing this book.

Introduction

There are no secrets to success. It is the result of
preparation, hard work, and learning from failure.

—Colin Powell [1]

I've written this book with the hope that it will serve as my lifetime
technical contribution to my database administrator (DBA) brethren. It
contains the sum knowledge and wisdom I've gathered this past
decade, both working on and speaking about data warehousing. It does
so purely from the DBA's perspective, solely for the DBA's needs and
benefit.

While I've worked on many data warehousing projects, my three
years at Electronic Data Systems (EDS) as the lead DBA for 7-
Eleven Corporation's enterprise data warehouse provided my greatest
learning experience. 7-Eleven is a world leader in convenience retail-
ing, with over 21,000 stores worldwide. The 7-Eleven enterprise data
warehouse:

*   Is multi-terabyte in size, with tables having hundreds of millions or
    billions of rows.

---

[1] *The Leadership Secret of Colin Powell*, Oren Harari (New York: McGraw-Hill, 2002).

- Is a true star schema design based on accurate business criteria and requirements.
- Has average and maximum report runtimes of seven minutes and four hours, respectively.
- Is operational 16X6 (i.e. the database is available 16 hours per day, 6 days per week).
- Has base data and aggregations that are no more than 24 hours old (i.e., updated daily).

While the 7-Eleven enterprise data warehouse may sound impressive, it was not that way from Day One. We started with Oracle 7.2 and a small Hewlett–Packard (HP) K-class server. We felt like genuine explorers as we charted new territory for both EDS and 7-Eleven. There were few reference books or white papers at that time with any detailed data warehousing techniques. Plus, there were few DBAs who had already successfully built multi-terabyte data warehouses with whom to network. Fortunately, EDS and 7-Eleven recognized this fact and embraced the truly iterative nature of data warehousing development.

Since you are reading this book, it's safe to assume we can agree that data warehousing is radically different than traditional online transaction processing (OLTP) applications. Whereas OLTP database and application development is generally well-defined and thus easy to control via policies and procedures, data warehousing is more iterative and experimental. You need the freedom, support, and longevity to intelligently experiment ad-infinitum. With few universal golden rules to apply, often the method of finding what works best for a given data warehouse is to:

- Brainstorm for design or tuning ideas.
- Add those ideas to a persistent list of ideas.
- Try whichever ideas currently look promising.
- Record a history of ideas attempted and their results.
- Keep one good idea out of 10–20 tried per iteration.
- Repeat the cycle with an ever growing list of new ideas …

As Thomas Peters states, "Life is pretty simple: You do some stuff. Most fails. Some works. You do more of what works."[2] That's some of the best advice I can recommend for successfully building a data warehouse as well.

PURPOSE

There are numerous data warehousing books out there, so why is this one different? Simply put: its DBA focus on implementation details. In fact, the mission statement for this book is:

To serve as the DBA's definitive and detailed reference regarding the successful design, construction, tuning, and maintenance of star schema data warehouses in Oracle 8i and 9i.

So how is this different from what's already out there? In general, I've found that most data warehousing books fall into one of three categories:

- **Conceptual**—Primarily educational about theories and practices, with very high-level information
- **Overview**—Catalogs of hardware, software, and database options, with few specific recommendations
- **Cookbook**—Detailed, DBA-oriented advice for all the data warehouse development lifecycle stages

Respectively, "best-of-breed" examples for these three categories are:

- *Data Warehouse Tool Kit: Practical Techniques for Building Dimensional Data Warehouses* by Ralph Kimball
- *Oracle8 Data Warehousing* by Gary Dodge and Tim Gorman
- This book, primarily since no other book exists with this kind of detailed DBA advice

---

[2.] *In Search of Excellence: Lessons from America's Best-Run Companies*, Thomas J. Peters and Robert H. Waterman, Jr. (New York: HarperCollins, 1982).

I mean no disrespect to these other categories or their books. I highly recommend Kimball's book to anyone new to data warehousing. And until such time as this books debuts, I also highly recommend Dodge's book for DBAs.

AUDIENCE

This book is intended for physical DBAs—period, end of story. This book assumes an extensive and detailed working knowledge of Oracle technologies. Moreover, it presumes a keen awareness of hardware and software options—often a skill possessed only by DBAs who also serve as at least the backup operating system (OS) administrator as well. That said, there are chapters that will be both applicable and beneficial to other members of the data warehousing team.

The sections on data modeling define how a DBA should interpret and extrapolate an entity relationship diagram (ERD) into a physical database design. So, this chapter would assist data modelers and application architects to understand how a DBA uses their input to create the underlying database structure.

Likewise, the sections on staging, promoting, and aggregating data define how a DBA should manage objects and processes to most expeditiously load massive amounts of data. So, this chapter would be both educational and inspirational to extract, transform, and load (ETL) programmers tasked with loading a data warehouse.

And finally, the chapter on querying the data defines the indices, statistics, and plans necessary to deliver the best possible ad-hoc query runtimes. So, this chapter would assist business intelligence front-end designers, who can appreciate how the database handles their complex, ad-hoc queries.

What Is a Data Warehouse?

Congratulations—you've joined a team either building or about to build a data warehouse. Do you really know what you've gotten yourself into? This may seem like a stupid question, but I've found that what people call a data warehouse varies significantly. In fact so much so, that I treat the term "data warehouse" with deep suspicion. I apologize for being so skeptical, but I've found that over 90% of what people call a data warehouse is open for debate! How do you tell someone his or her data warehouse is not really one without starting a fight?

A few years ago, there was no such thing as data warehousing. Now we hear about data warehouses everywhere and everyone seems to be building them. Success stories abound in technical and business journals. Many database conferences now have a data warehousing track or special interest group (SIG). Moreover, businesspeople have bought into them "hook, line, and sinker." They all want data warehouses and data marts. Now, they even want them via the Web! These are most often referred to as Web houses. That's the good news—there's plenty of demand.

But, demand for something by itself is not sufficient justification. For example, I would like to retire from the workforce right now. But as my wife kindly reminds me, it does not make sense given our financial reserves. Far too often, I've seen data warehouses being built for all the wrong reasons:

- Businesspeople ask for one since it's in vogue to have one.
- The chief information officer (CIO) decides to sponsor a data warehousing project initiative.
- Information Systems (IS) management submits a data warehousing proposal for funding.
- IS management combines several reporting systems into a warehouse.
- IS management renames an existing reporting system a data warehouse.

The point is that a true data warehouse should solve a genuine business need and thus be sponsored by the businesspeople who will benefit from it. Moreover, a true data warehouse follows some very specific design guidelines we'll be discussing in this book. Something is not a data warehouse simply because someone wants it to be or says it is.

Why am I making such a fuss over this? It's actually quite simple. The techniques espoused in this book will only work for genuine data warehouses. These exact same techniques will either not work or actually make things worse for entities that are not data warehouses. As such, this chapter is actually quite critical in terms of your data warehouse's success.

THE NATURE OF THE BEAST

So just how do you decide if you're working on a true data warehouse? First, examine the intended nature of your database and the application it supports. For each subject area in your data warehouse, simply ask your sponsoring business user to provide the following eight items:

- Mission statement
- Number of ad-hoc query users
- Number ad-hoc queries per day per ad-hoc user
- Number of pre-canned report users
- Number of pre-canned reports per day per pre-canned user
- Number of pre-canned reports

- Amount of history to keep in months, quarters, or years
- Typical daily, weekly, or monthly volume of data to record

These answers should help you categorize your database application into one of the following choices:

- Online transaction processing (OLTP)
- Operational data store (ODS)
- Online analytical processing (OLAP)
- Data mart/data warehouse (DM/DW)

Use the criteria outlined in Table 1–1 to make your distinction.

Table 1–1   General Database Application Categorizations

	OLTP	ODS	OLAP	DM / DW
Business Focus	Operational	Operational / Tactical	Tactical	Tactical / Strategic
End User Tools	Client/Server or Web	Client/Server or Web	Client/Server	Client/Server or Web
DB Technology	Relational	Relational	Cubic	Relational
Transaction Count	Large	Medium	Small	Small
Transaction Size	Small	Medium	Medium	Large
Transaction Time	Short	Medium	Medium	Long
DB Size in GB	10–400	100–800	100–800	800—80,000
Data Modeling	Traditional ERD	Traditional ERD	N/A	Dimensional
Normalization	3–5 NF[1]	3 NF	N/A	0 NF

1. Normal Form

For example, suppose your answers are as follows:

- "The point of sale (POS) subject area of the data warehouse should enable executives and senior sales managers to perform predictive, "what-if" sales analysis and historical analysis of:
  - A sales campaign's effectiveness
  - Geographic sales patterns

- • Calendar sales patterns
- • The effects of weather on sales
- 20 ad-hoc query users
- 10–20 ad-hoc queries a day per ad-hoc user
- 40 pre-canned report users
- 1–4 pre-canned reports a day per pre-canned user
- 60 months of history
- 40 million sales transactions per day

From this example, we can discern that we genuinely have a candidate for a data mart or data warehouse. First, the mission statement clearly indicates that our users' requirements are of a more tactical or strategic nature. Second, the majority of our report executions will clearly be ad-hoc (200–400 ad-hoc versus a maximum of 160 pre-canned). Third, we have significant historical data requirements and large amounts of raw data—and thus a potentially very large database (especially once we consider aggregates as well).

While it may seem like I've painted an example tailored to the conclusion, I've actually found the process to be this straightforward and easy in most cases. Unfortunately, these days, people tend to call any reporting database a data warehouse. It's okay for people to call their projects whatever they like, but as I pointed out, the techniques in this book only apply to the DM/DW column of Table 1–1.

DATA WAREHOUSE VS. BIG DATABASE

One of the key mistakes people make is labeling their database as a data warehouse solely based on its size. Over the past decade, three phenomena have occurred resulting in major increases in average database size:

- • The cost of space versus the value of the data has decreased.
- • Companies now value the data as a critical business asset.
- • Companies have merged into large multi-national entities.

In other words, the cost of keeping data online is cheap, the perceived value of that data is now very high, and the size of companies and their data needs have grown. As such, many of today's OLTP and ODS databases routinely grow into the 100–800 gigabyte (GB) range. But that does not make them data warehouses. For example, SAP and PeopleSoft enterprise resource planning (ERP) databases of 400 GB or more are not uncommon, yet they are not data warehouses, even at these extremely large sizes. Remember, size alone does not a data warehouse make.

The simplest way to avoid labeling a large database as a data warehouse is to add some DBA-centric questions and answers to the description of the nature of that database. For each subject area in your data warehouse, simply ask the physical DBA to provide estimates for the following seven items:

- The number of tables
- Average big table row count
- Average big table size in GB
- Largest table's row count
- Largest table's size in GB
- Largest transaction rollback needed in GB
- Largest temporary segment needed in GB

Data warehouses generally have fewer, larger tables, whereas non-data warehouse databases usually possess more, smaller tables. Of additional interest are the temporary and rollback segment needs of the database. Data warehouses tend to need them as large as the largest object (for rebuilds), whereas non-data warehouse databases only need them large enough for the largest transaction.

Use the criteria outlined in Table 1–2 for your evaluation.

Table 1–2   General Database Application Characteristics

	OLTP	ODS	OLAP	DM / DW
Number of Tables	100–1000's	100–1000's	10–100's	10–100's
Average Table's Row Count	10's of Thousands	10's of Thousands	10–100's of Millions	100–1000's of Millions
Average Table's Size in GB	10's of MB	10's of MB	10's of GB	10–100's of GB

Table 1–2   General Database Application Characteristics (Continued)

	OLTP	ODS	OLAP	DM / DW
Largest Table's Row Count	10–100's of Millions	10–100's of Millions	10–100's of Millions	100–10,000's of Millions
Largest Table's Size in GB	10's of GB	10's of GB	10's of GB	10–100's of GB
Rollback Segment's Size in GB	100's of MB	100's of MB	N/A	10–100's of GB
Temp Segment's Size in GB	100's of MB	100's of MB	N/A	10–100's of GB

Continuing with our previous example, suppose your requirements are as follows:

- 8 tables
- 500 million rows per big table
- 50 GB per big table
- 2 billion rows for largest table
- 160 GB for largest table
- 160 GB to rebuild largest table
- 60 GB to rebuild largest index

From this example, we can again discern that we have a data mart or data warehouse. First, we have very few tables. A typical OLTP or ERP database would have hundreds or even thousands of tables. Second, the row counts of our smallest big table and largest table have the right order of magnitude. Row counts expressed with lots of zeros or in powers of ten greater than ten (e.g., 10^{10}) are more likely to be in data warehouses. Finally, look at our rollback and temporary segments' needs. They're as big as some entire databases!

While it may seem like I've once again painted an example tailored to the conclusion, I've actually found the process to be this straightforward and easy in most cases as well. Unfortunately, these days, people tend to call any very large database a data warehouse. Once again, it's okay for people to call their projects whatever they like. But as pointed out, the techniques in this book only apply to the DM/DW column of Table 1–2.

OPERATIONAL DATA STORES DON'T COUNT

Frequently people don't understand why an ODS is not a data warehouse. Since many ODS projects are referred to as data warehousing initiatives, people often mistakenly assume that an ODS is therefore a data warehouse. That assumption is false as an ODS is merely a stepping-stone to a true data warehouse. An ODS is simply a means to an end, and not the end itself. Let's see where the ODS fits into the data warehousing equation.

Companies generally have numerous legacy application systems that were developed with varying technologies over a long period of time. For example, an insurance company may have different policy and commission applications across its different business units (e.g., life, health, property, casualty, and investments). It also would not be uncommon to have several such applications for the various product families within each different business unit (e.g., for investments, IRAs vs. annuities vs. 401Ks vs. 403Bs). Moreover, there could even be different applications by product nature (e.g., individual vs. group policies). So, an insurance company could have dozens of policy and commission applications across many different hardware and software platforms. Furthermore, these applications were very likely developed in total seclusion from the others. Thus, each application is really like an island unto itself (often referred to as stovepipe applications).

Now, imagine that you need to generate reports for a specific customer or agent, John Smith. Since John Smith the customer or agent might exist in one or more of those different applications, the insurance company needs a common staging area to merge this eclectic data into one centralized source. Such a centralized collection of disparate but interrelated data sources is known as an ODS. Figure 1–1 demonstrates a typical OD.

An ODS contains the centralized, single-source location for OLTP data. It is very often referred to as the system of record. Moreover, an ODS typically keeps a window of history on that data (usually by merely adding date and timestamp columns to the OLTP data). So, an ODS can be quite large, often into the 400+ GB range. But, ODS data is in its most raw form, sometimes nothing more than

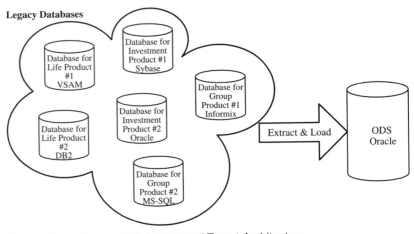

Figure 1–1   Typical ODS Source and Target Architecture

a copy of OLTP data with dates and timestamps. No useful transformations or aggregations have been performed to translate that transactional data into the tactical or strategic format necessary for executive management reporting needs. Therefore, to repetitively report off that ODS data in its unprocessed form would be very expensive. Thus, ODS data needs to be transformed into a format suitable for effective and efficient reporting. This pathway for loading a data warehouse via an ODS is shown in the highlighted portion of Figure 1–2.

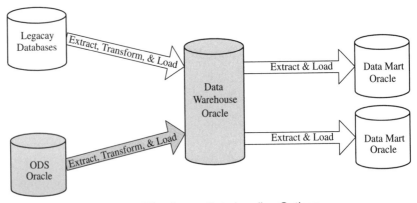

Figure 1–2   Typical Data Warehouse Data Loading Options

Also note that Figure 1–2 shows that you can just as easily bypass the ODS and directly transform legacy database data into the data warehouse. The point is that an ODS is not mandatory. For example, let's assume that we have a number of legacy application databases that were all developed in Oracle. Furthermore, let's assume that we have an accurate data dictionary for all business attributes such that all like tables and columns across those different Oracle databases have exactly the same type and size. In this case, building an ODS would merely serve to remove duplicate rows. In such a case, we might reasonably forgo building an ODS.

Figure 1–2 also shows that the data warehouse resides separately from the data marts. The point is that a data warehouse and a data mart are not quite the same thing. The primary difference between a data mart and a data warehouse is simply a question of scope. A data warehouse is a single, large store for the transformation of all legacy databases or ODS data. So, everyone would report off an enterprise data warehouse. A data mart is a smaller, specialized store for the transformation of all related legacy databases and ODS data, generally referred to as a subject area. For example, a consumer retail company might keep a data mart of cash register or POS data. A typical company might then have several to several dozen such data marts.

EXECUTIVE INFORMATION SYSTEMS DON'T COUNT

Our original question was: What is a data warehouse? As we've discovered, it's a large, centralized, specialized database for doing data management and executive reporting. In the old days, we just called such databases executive information systems (EISs). A logical question is then: How is a data warehouse different from an EIS? While it may not be readily apparent, there are some key differences.

The primary difference is the intended audience. EISs were built just to support making tactical decisions, meaning they were used by mid-level management. But, an effective data warehouse will support both mid-level and true executive management for both tactical and strategic decisions. A data warehouse contains the data necessary to make decisions such as "Should we even be in this business?" and "Is the return on investment (ROI) of the current business the best we can do, or is there another business whose opportunity cost makes it worth considering?"

Another key difference is the method used to obtain that information. EISs generally provided mostly canned reports, with limited user-driven query capabilities. As such, tuning an EIS database was generally very straightforward. A data warehouse, on the other hand, possesses fewer canned reports—reports are mostly used for tactical decision-making. These strategic decisions require much more business-savvy user interaction. The user typically poses what-if scenarios to drill down to a conclusion. As such, tuning a data warehouse is a monumental challenge. The DBA must find a structure conducive to any number of unknown and often nightmarish queries.

By far, the biggest difference is the sheer magnitude in size difference between an EIS and data warehouse. The EIS databases preceded today's cheap hardware, so they tended to be on the same size scale as the OTLP systems from which they were derived. This indeed is quite important, because tuning a billion-row, multigigabyte table is a big challenge, even with today's super-fast hardware. In fact, yesteryears' database systems could not handle databases of this magnitude, let alone optimize queries against them.

So, data warehousing has genuinely become a market niche for any DBA. But, there is a price to be paid by DBAs making this switch, as they will find their OLTP skills and instincts will quickly erode. More importantly, other DBAs will find the data warehousing DBA to appear arrogant at times. Because, after dealing with billions of rows and hundreds of gigabytes to terabytes, how does one get excited about typical OLTP sizes? It's actually quite fun to sound like Carl Sagan and state: "My average table has billions and billions of rows..."

WAREHOUSES EVOLVE WITHOUT PHASES

The typical database application development life cycle is something like the following:

- Deliver a version.
- Begin work on the next version.

- Perform maintenance on the current version.
- Promote changes or deltas to the current version.
- Incorporate changes or deltas into the new version.
- Repeat the process.

For EDS and 7-Eleven, we had to have a customer signature and scheduled downtime to promote a database application change for any OLTP system. This practice makes good business sense. When OLTP systems run the customer's business, you don't want to make unapproved or unscheduled changes that could result in customer OLTP application downtime, because such downtime could cost the customer real money.

In data warehousing, things are very different. There really is no database application as the database itself is the object of desire from the customer's viewpoint. The data warehouse may be queried by end-user tools and have batch programs for loading, but the database itself is really the heart and soul of the data warehouse. Customers see its information at their disposal as the real deliverable. Or, as I sometimes like to say, "It's the database, Stupid."

As users mine the data warehouse to answer new and more involved business questions, they quite often and regularly find something lacking. The most common requests are often to add a new column to a table or create a new summarization or aggregate table that does not exist. The first solves a missing data problem and the second reduces report runtimes. In addition, users often ask for columns to be displayed differently or contain additional data. The point is that change requests come in daily, from mid-level managers to true executives.

So, the data warehousing application development lifecycle looks more like:

- Deliver the first version.
- Promote changes or deltas to the current version.
- Repeat the process.

This evolutionary method actually requires a much more cautious approach to promoting changes. The batch load programmers, the DBA, and the project manager must all be 100% in sync with each other at all times because there is no real version control of the code or database data definition language (DDL) to fall back on. Data warehouse changes occur with too much frequency and urgency to follow a strict development methodology. From the OLTP perspective, the data warehouse team appears to fly by the seat of their pants. So, a great project manager, a detail-oriented project lead, and a very experienced DBA are needed to make this process work.

THE WAREHOUSE ROLLER COASTER

Finally, I want to remind the reader of the enormous challenges for any data warehousing DBA. I often reminisce about the past decade and feel that Dickens' "It was the best of times, it was the worst of times" best describes my data warehousing experiences. Be prepared as a data warehousing DBA to experience little joy from few wins and a lot of agony from numerous defeats. With so few Golden Rules and fellow data warehousing DBAs in existence, expect more of the latter. But remember that if you don't succeed at first, try, try again. It's taken me nearly 20 years of working with Oracle and 10 years of data warehousing experience to feel like anything more than a base novice. There is no shame in making mistakes in data warehousing. In fact, it's the only proven method to finding the best solutions. Or, as Babe Ruth once said, "Every strike brings me closer to the next home run."

Software Architecture

Note that unlike other data warehousing and general DBA books, I've placed the software architecture chapter prior to the chapter on hardware architecture. That's because I see this as a fundamental problem with the other offerings. If you'll indulge me for a simple analogy: Why buy a gas stove if you're attempting to cook microwave dinners? You need a destination before you set out. You need a goal before you try to achieve. That's just how it's done.

Remember the following old adage: Don't put the cart before the horse? Well, far too often, that's what happens with Oracle database applications, including data warehouses. That is, technical management succumbs to both hardware and software vendor recommendations before the application's true software architecture has been adequately defined. Often, the rationale is that the hardware must be ordered prior to the project so that it's available for the team to work on; otherwise, they'd be sitting around idle. Hogwash! One of the initial team's jobs should be to define both the software and hardware architectures. A common mistake is to assume that the project proposal has adequate insight into what's truly needed.

For example, our initial hardware selection for the 7-Eleven data warehouse was a Hewlett-Packard (HP) K-class server with a small EMC disk array. Oracle and HP sold our technical management on the idea of using Oracle Parallel Server (OPS) and adding 4–6 small central processing unit (CPU) servers as needed. To our management, this seemed like a reasonable recommendation. As for the vendors, knowing the information they were given, this was probably quite fitting. Less than a year later, both the K-class server and EMC disk array were donated to another OLTP project. We had outgrown that hardware. But more importantly, it did not fit into our software architecture. We had to buy all new hardware to continue. Plus, we never used OPS, and we switched from the raw files required by OPS to the Veritas file system with Quick IO. In short, we switched just about everything possible.

So what happened? In short, management went to the vendors and said we're building a data warehouse and we've got this much to spend—what should we buy? What do other people like us buy? Don't get me wrong, though. Those vendors were doing us a great service by making such recommendations. But, their recommendations should have been viewed as defining the universe of products for consideration. Ultimately, the data warehouse DBA must be the one who defines the software architecture. Then, he or she must go to the vendors of choice, show them the proposed software architecture, and ask what hardware they have that fits your requirements. You'll find at least two things to be true. First, they'll recommend fewer solutions as possibilities. And second, with more insight, their recommendations will be much better. Hence, you should not have to change everything (as we did) a year later.

Another way to view the software architecture is to treat it like a logical data model for your hardware needs. Thus, the software architecture defines the database and application design concepts that you're embracing. The hardware architecture represents a particular instantiation of the equipment necessary to fulfill those needs. And, like data modeling, there may be more than one way to physically implement your logical model. In other words, you may have more than one hardware solution that can get the job done.

As with many endeavors, it helps to know your options. In other words, to pick a solution, it helps to know the available possibilities. You still have to pick the correct one from among the choices available, but at least you won't have missed possible good choices by not knowing of their existence. So, we must examine an eclectic collection of software architecture options. Some are related; others are not. But it's the sum of the selections that will help you define your ultimate software architecture. Armed with that information, you can proceed on to the next chapter and correctly select your hardware architecture.

BUSINESS INTELLIGENCE OPTIONS

There are many business intelligence tools out there, but as the DBA, it should not be your job to select one—just to support it. However, that means that you'll need a basic understanding of its architecture, resource requirements, database connection model, query construction techniques, query tuning capabilities, and numerous other aspects that will influence your software architecture definition.

There are three basic business intelligence software questions to ask:

- Will the business intelligence user interface be fat or thin? (Will there be a web server?)
- Will the business intelligence application be two- or three-tier? (Will there be an application server?)
- If there are web and/or application server components, what operating system (OS) platforms are supported?

Often, the end-users' business intelligence software selection and/or general user interface preferences will decide the first two issues for you. While this may seem like an oversimplification, the answers to these two questions can yield many different results. Assuming that typical data warehousing business intelligence software users have Intel-based personal computers (PCs) running Microsoft Windows, then the four most common possibilities include (shown in Figure 2–1):

- PC to database server(s)
- PC to application server to database server(s)
- PC to Web server to database server(s)
- PC to Web server to application server to database server(s)

Of course, the Web and application server components could be on the same physical box as the database server. This diagram was meant merely to show the logical concept of all the possible components and their interrelationships.

Although there are numerous architectural designs for both Web and application servers, the key issue for any DBA is the Web and/or application server's process model. Common process models include:

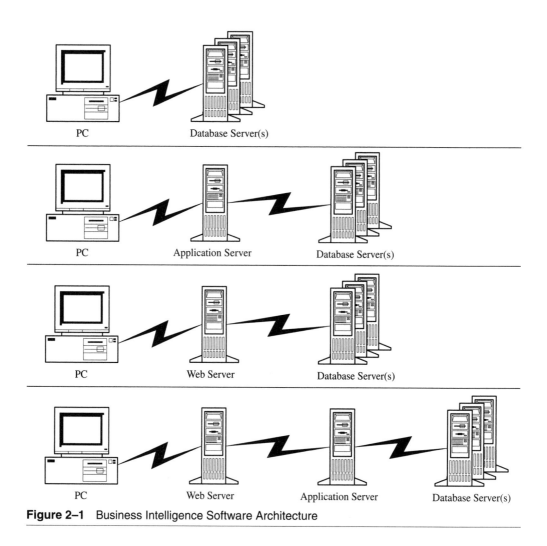

Figure 2–1   Business Intelligence Software Architecture

- Single-process/single-thread with blocking input/output (I/O)
- Single-process/single-thread with non-blocking I/O
- Process per request
- Process pool
- Thread per request
- Thread pool

The ramifications for the DBA are in the volume and nature of the corresponding database server processes. These characteristics can affect the DBA's decision regarding Oracle's process model for issues such as:

- Connection pooling
- Multi-threaded server (MTS)
- Parallel query option (PQO)
- OPS or real application clusters (RAC)

Let's examine a simple, yet realistic example. The selected business intelligence software requires an application server. Typically, the business intelligence front-end constructs a report definition that the application server then processes. But, a single business intelligence report may in fact possess dozens of individual structured query language (SQL) queries, which the application server submits to the database and then coalesces into actual reports. Moreover, the application server submits all those requests simultaneously using a process per request process model. In addition, a single business intelligence user may submit multiple report requests concurrently. So, a single business intelligence end-user may in fact represent hundreds of simultaneous database connections!

We're not done yet with this example. Let's also assume that the application server can only run on a Windows NT server while the database platform will be UNIX. That's a "boatload" of network traffic described above between these two servers. So, it would probably be advisable to put the two servers on a dedicated, isolated fiber network connection. Are you now beginning to see how the software architecture drives the hardware selection process?

ORACLE VERSION OPTIONS

Far too often, people have the expectation that using expensive hardware is the only way to obtain optimal performance from their data warehouse. They'll spend a lot of money to throw both hardware and software at their performance problems, including items such as:

- More memory
- Faster CPUs
- Newer CPUs
- 64-bit CPUs
- Multi-CPU servers (symmetric multi-processing [SMP] or massively parallel processing [MPP])
- 64-bit UNIX
- 64-bit Oracle
- RAID disk arrays (storage area network [SAN] or network-attached storage [NAS])
- More disk array memory cache
- Faster disk drives (e.g., 15,000 RPM)
- More disks (i.e., switch RAID-5 to RAID-1+0)
- RAW [1] devices
- Better file systems (e.g., Veritas with Quick IO option)

I've seen more money spent on hardware upgrades to solve performance problems in data warehousing than on any other item. One company with a data warehouse I visited actually switched both its UNIX server and disk array vendors in an attempt to solve its severe performance problems. Imagine their surprise when the problem did not go away with all that new hardware. Then imagine their utter surprise when it was fixable in a couple of hours merely by changing a few INIT.ORA parameters and redoing their table and index statistics collections!

In reality, the correct Oracle version, proper use of all its features, and the underlying database design are the most important factors for obtaining optimal performance for any successful data warehouse implementation. Of course, there are certain minimum

---

[1] There are two common kinds of operating file systems: cooked and raw. With cooked file systems, the operating system manages access and operations on files and their contents. With raw file systems, the applications themselves do this work—bypassing the operating system file system.

hardware and software requirements that must be met. For example, I cannot imagine a multi-terabyte data warehouse on a PC. I also cannot envision a successful data warehouse on a mainframe—if it's using the wrong version of Oracle or fails to utilize Oracle's data warehousing-specific features.

The primary database feature requirements for a successful Oracle data warehouse are:

- Reliable and efficient partitioning
- Reliable and efficient bitmap indexes
- Query explain plan support for star transformation access method
- Reliable and efficient statistics for cost-based optimization
- Reliable and efficient histograms for cost-based optimization
- Reliable, efficient, and easy-to-use parallel query and data manipulation language (DML)

Let's see how the various Oracle versions measure up.

Oracle 7.X lacks all the key data warehousing feature requirements. You do not want to be on this version for any kind of serious data warehousing project. You will fail or have to upgrade once your data warehouse exceeds a few hundred GB. For example, a simple data warehouse query that ran over 13 hours under Oracle 7.3 ran in less than 10 minutes under Oracle 8.0, in less than 7 minutes under Oracle 8i, and in less than 5 minutes under Oracle 9i. Except for minor INIT.ORA changes, the only difference was the optimizer's chosen explain plan for the query.

Still not convinced? Let's examine the features people think exist in 7.X that make data warehouses a possibility:

- Oracle 7.X's partitioning is really what's referred to as partition views. It's nothing more than a way to have a view definition tie together disjointed tables so as to give the appearance of partitioning. Partition views lack partition-based DML operations, partition-level query options, and partition-based indexing. Partition views are smoke and mirrors at best trying to resemble real partitioning. They don't cut it.

- Oracle 7.X's bitmap indexes are totally unreliable. I logged so many TARs[2] on bitmap indexes under both Oracle 7.X and 8.0 that I almost gave up on using them. Thank goodness 8i and 9i fixed these problems. If you like ORA-600 errors and wrong results, then by all means use bitmap indexes on large tables under Oracle 7.X.

- Oracle 7.X's STAR hint is also a joke. It does a Cartesian product of all the dimension tables and then joins that to the fact table. The thought was that doing one join was the way to go. And if I've got to actually convince you that Cartesian products are undesirable, then you're reading the wrong book.

Oracle 8.0 is the first Oracle version to meet many of the data warehousing feature requirements. But like new cars, the first model year or two are often worth avoiding. The partitioning is fairly sound, but the bitmap indexes remain problematic. Specifically, it seems that bitmap indexes on tables with over a few hundred million rows still raise a few ORA-600 errors and the occasional wrong result. If you must build a data warehouse under Oracle 8.0, then be advised that it will work best only for very small data warehouses.

Both Oracle 8i and 9i support all the data warehousing feature requirements. I've found both Oracle 8.1.7 and 9.0.1 to make data warehousing projects more likely to succeed—so much so that my advice is that you should only make an attempt at a data warehouse in these versions of Oracle, period. Now, many people might state that their ERP applications are still on Oracle 7.3 and their core business OLTP applications are primarily on Oracle 8.0—with a few smaller projects underway on either Oracle 8i or 9i. So what? The data warehouse is a new project and must have those features in the newer releases to succeed.

Here's another piece of advice that will sound hard to accept: Successful data warehouses rely so heavily on these new features that their DBAs tend to ride the bleeding edge of Oracle releases. For example, my 7-Eleven data warehouse was considered a huge success by any and all measures. Guess what? We were never more than

---

[2]When you call Oracle technical support and log an issue or bug, you are given a TAR number to reference the occasion. TAR stands for technical assistance requests.

60 days out on any major upgrade or patch, ever. Yes, the rest of 7-Eleven was still on 7.3 and working on a phased plan to upgrade the ERP and OLTP systems over the following year to Oracle 8i. But, the data warehouse had already been on Oracle 8i (and its latest release) for over a year. In fact, we were already planning for Oracle 9i.

Another way to look at this is to review the market thrusts of both Oracle 8i and 9i. Each version, when released, included new key features primarily for two very hot market niches: the Web and data warehousing. The "Getting to Know Oracle 8i" document (Oracle Part #A68020-01) states that:

> Oracle8i, the database for Internet computing, changes the way information is managed and accessed to meet the demands of the Internet age, while providing significant new features for traditional online transaction processing (OLTP) and data warehouse applications. It provides advanced tools to manage all types of data in Web sites, but it also delivers the performance, scalability, and availability needed to support very large database (VLDB) and mission-critical applications.

In the same document under data warehousing improvements, Oracle states:

- In the Oracle8 Enterprise Edition, a new method for executing star queries has been introduced. Using a more efficient algorithm, and utilizing bitmapped indexes, the new star-query processing provides a significant performance boost to data warehouse applications.
- Insert, update, and delete operations can now be run in parallel in the Oracle8 Enterprise Edition. These operations, known as parallel DML, are executed in parallel across multiple processes. By having these operations execute in parallel, the statement will be completed much more quickly than if the same statement were executed in a serial fashion. Parallel DML complements parallel query by providing parallel transaction execution as well as queries. Parallel DML is useful in a decision support (DSS) or data warehouse environment where bulk DML operations are common. However, parallel DML operations can also speed up batch jobs running in an OLTP database.

- The Oracle8 Enterprise Edition can manage databases of hundreds of terabytes in size because of partitioning, administrative improvements, and internal enhancements. Many size limitations in earlier versions of Oracle have been raised, such as the number of columns per table, the maximum database size, and the number of files per database.

Likewise, "Oracle9i Database New Features" [Oracle Part #A90120-02] states:

Oracle9i broadens the footprint of the relational database in a data warehouse by becoming a scalable data engine for all operations on data warehousing data, and not just in loading and basic query operations. As such, it is the first true data warehouse platform. Oracle9i provides new server functionality in analytic capabilities, ETL (Extraction, Transformation, Loading), and data mining.

Moreover, "Oracle9i Database 9.2 New Features" [Oracle Part #A96531-01] states:

Oracle9i release 2 continues to challenge the competition by providing the best platform support for business intelligence in medium to large-scale enterprises. Oracle9i technology focuses especially on the challenges raised by the large volume of data and the need for near real time complex analysis in an Internet-enabled environment.

It should be clear that Oracle 8i and 9i are clearly targeted for the world of data warehousing.

ORACLE INSTANCE OPTIONS—QUERYING

The first key architectural issue the DBA must decide is how many Oracle instances will form the data warehouse for the purpose of supporting business intelligence queries? In essence, the DBA must decide how he or she will partition the data across instances. In fact, the answer to this one question alone will do more to define the available software and hardware architectural options open to the DBA than anything else.

For example, putting the entire data warehouse all in one instance will probably require a mainframe-like platform, whereas separating subject areas across instances will permit the DBA to use lots of smaller servers. Of course, it's really how the business users need access to the data that drives this decision. If your users must have access to all the subject areas, then separation may in fact make using the warehouse less simple.

Let's agree on some terminology to assist this discussion. If we use the term "data warehouse," or "DW," let's take that to mean the entire scope of all the subject areas. If we use the term "data mart," or "DM," let's take that to mean a subset of all the subject areas. Using these terms, let's examine our Oracle architecture options.

For those building an enterprise data warehouse, the options are (shown in Figure 2–2):

- Option 1—Entire DW in a single database, with a single instance, on a single server
- Option 2—Entire DW in a single database, with multiple instances, on a single server
- Option 3—Entire DW in a single database, with multiple instances, on multiple servers

Note that the second option does not make much sense, unless you have a very large database server with an OS that supports partitioning of the hardware. Also note that both the second and third options require the use of OPS or RAC (OPS/RAC).

For those with separate and distinct data marts, the options are (shown in Figure 2–3):

- Option 1—All DMs in separate databases, with multiple instances, on a single server
- Option 2—All DMs in separate databases, with multiple instances, on multiple servers

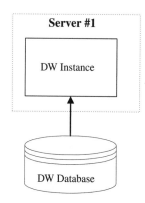

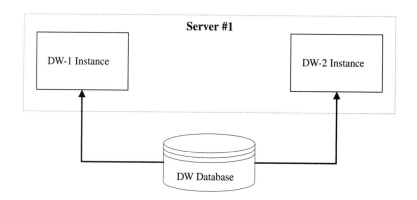

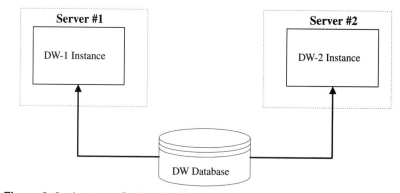

Figure 2–2   Instance Options for Enterprise Data Warehouse

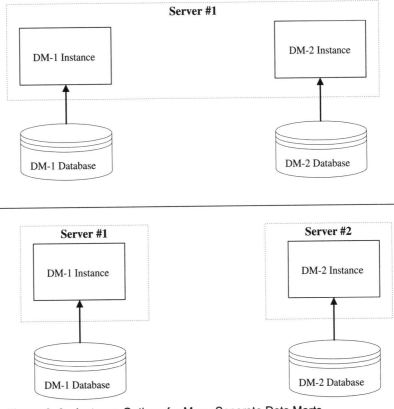

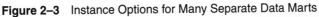

Figure 2–3 Instance Options for Many Separate Data Marts

Note that the first option does not make much sense, unless you have a very large database server with an OS that supports partition-ing of the hardware.

Of these database architectures, OPS/RAC is probably the least understood. In simple terms, OPS/RAC permits more than one instance (both the System Global Area [SGA] and processes) to con-nect to the same database (files). The instances can be on one or more heterogeneous servers; the only requirement is the ability to share one common file system.

OPS/RAC offers many potential advantages, including:

- Load balancing
- Fault tolerance

- Scalability
- Flexibility

However, these advantages come with some serious costs, including:

- Tougher to administer the OS
- Requires use of RAW devices
- Tougher to administer the database
- Tougher to diagnose/tune the database
- Tougher to backup/recover the database
- Generates more network traffic (i.e., inter-instance pinging)
- Limited maximum CPU power per DM or subject area
- Smaller pool of OPS/RAC qualified OS and DBA candidates

ORACLE INSTANCE OPTIONS—LOADING

The second key Oracle architectural issue the DBA must determine is how many Oracle instances will form the data warehouse for the purpose of loading data? This definition may seem less clear than the previous one regarding queries, but actually it's a much simpler question: Will the data warehouse data be loaded in one step or two?

There are only two options here (shown in Figure 2–4):

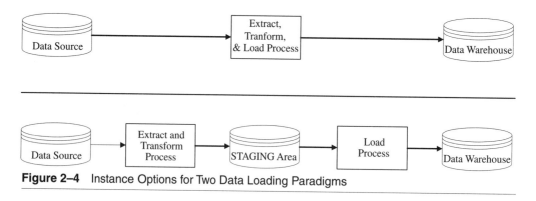

Figure 2–4   Instance Options for Two Data Loading Paradigms

- Option 1—Load the data from the source directly into the query tables
- Option 2—Load the data from the source into a staging area first, then into the query tables

The first method requires direct access to the live data warehouse tables, which very often is quite undesirable. For example, the data load process may involve numerous complex extract, transform, and load (ETL) operations that can consume significantly more time than simply loading the data. Since many data warehouses have very limited batch windows in which to load their data, both the extract and transform operations may need to be performed outside those batch windows. So, it is not uncommon to separate the overall ETL process through the use of a staging area.

Staging tables typically hold up to a few batch cycles' worth of data. For example, a data warehouse fact table might have a billion rows and load 10 million new records per night. Assuming that a batch loading cycle is successfully completed at least once every three days, the staging tables would hold anywhere from 10–30 million rows. Once a batch cycle completes, the staging area tables are simply truncated.

The staging approach offers several interesting advantages. First, the DBA can implement referential integrity (i.e., foreign keys) and other database constraints to enforce the data's accuracy. These constraint mechanisms do not seriously degrade the load time for tables under 100 million rows. This is key since it's easier to define such value checks once in the database rather than expecting each and every program to properly code all such validations.

Second, if the transform or extract process aborts or errors out, the DBA can simply truncate the staging tables and restart the requisite batch jobs. This ability to simply reset and restart is sufficient reason to embrace this method. In essence, it's like having a super-commit or rollback mechanism for the data loading process.

Third, the DBA can better manage disk space allocations. The staging tables are sized for one to N batch cycles' worth of data, whereas the data warehouse fact tables are sized for much longer time intervals (e.g., weekly, monthly, or quarterly). Additionally, only a handful of simpler load programs require access to the actual data warehouse fact tables. The bulk of the more complex extract and transform programs don't access the actual data warehouse fact tables, merely the staging tables.

Finally, the staging approach also offers an extremely wide range of database implementations. Keep in mind that all the options discussed below go hand in hand with your prior database architecture decisions for queries.

Next, there are options to consider if the data warehouse and staging tables will be in the same instance, including (shown in Figure 2–5):

- Option 1—DW and STAGING in a single database, with a single instance, on a single server
- Option 2—DW and STAGING in a single database, with multiple instances, on a single server
- Option 3—DW and STAGING in a single database, with multiple instances, on multiple servers

Note that the second option does not make much sense unless you have a very large database server with an OS that supports partitioning of the hardware. Also note that both the second and third options require the use of OPS/RAC.

The first option, combining the data warehouse and staging table access in a single instance accessing a common database on a single database server, offers the greatest simplicity. This is probably the best-known and most widely used Oracle software architecture out there. But, combining such radically different tables in one database instance has some severe tuning drawbacks. How do you best size the INIT.ORA parameters that control the SGA to simultaneously support reporting and data loading needs? You sure don't want to have to shut down and restart the database to change those parameters every time you switch between these needs. And what if these needs overlap? How do you set those parameters to best suit concurrently running reports and loading data, especially when reports are highly affected by database buffer cache hit ratios, and data loads tend to saturate that cache? Thus, loading data while running reports within a single database instance will just make the reports run that much slower. Of course, there is also the issue of sharing other server resources during

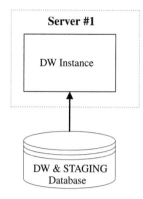

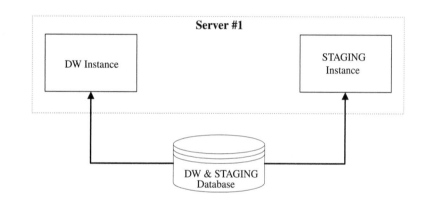

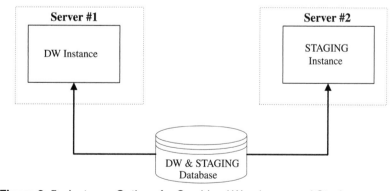

Figure 2–5   Instance Options for Combined Warehouse and Staging

concurrent report and data load execution, but the decreased database buffer cache hit ratio will be the most noticeable.

The second option, separating the data warehouse and staging table access across multiple instances accessing a common database on a single database server, solves the problems of the first option, but introduces issues of its own. Since many server operating systems limit the total amount of shared memory that can be allocated for the SGA, splitting the database instances would require defining smaller, fixed SGA memory allocations whose cumulative size fits within that limit. For example, some 32-bit operating systems limit the total SGA size to 1.7 GB. So, the DBA might allocate 1.2 GB to the DW SGA and 500 MB to the STAGING SGA. But in effect, that translates to 500 MB of wasted (i.e., lost) memory when reports are running and data loads are not, and, an enormous 1.2 GB of waste when data loads are running and reports are not. Plus, the programs that promote data from the STAGING instance to the DW instance would have to communicate over an Oracle DBLINK, which is not as fast as the inter-instance operations of the first option.

Moreover, all the ETL programs (refer back to Figure 2–4) would have to be designed and deployed correctly. The extract and transform programs should connect to and process against the STAGING instance, period, whereas the load programs should connect to and process against the DW instance while reading data from the STAGING instance via an Oracle DBLINK. Otherwise, two-phase commits (2PCs) will enter the performance equation and slow data loading operations down by orders of magnitude.

The correct SQL to connect to and process against the DW instance while reading data from the STAGING instance via an Oracle DBLINK without 2PCs is:

```
INSERT INTO WAREHOUSE_TABLE
SELECT * FROM STAGING_TABLE@STAGING_INSTANCE
```

The incorrect SQL to connect to and process against the STAGING instance while writing data to the DW instance via an Oracle DBLINK with 2PCs is:

```
INSERT INTO WAREHOUSE_TABLE@DW_INSTANCE
SELECT * FROM STAGING_TABLE
```

The third option, separating the data warehouse and staging table access across multiple instances accessing a common database across multiple database servers, solves the OS limits for shared memory problem, but requires two or more servers and increases network traffic between them. The primary advantage is that both the DW and STAGING servers' capacity can be selected to best match their respective roles. However, in the long run, buying two smaller servers will generally cost more than buying one larger server with the same overall capacity. Furthermore, the network connections between those servers should be ultra-high–speed, and preferably dedicated.

There are yet more options if the data warehouse and staging tables will be separate instances, including (shown in Figure 2–6):

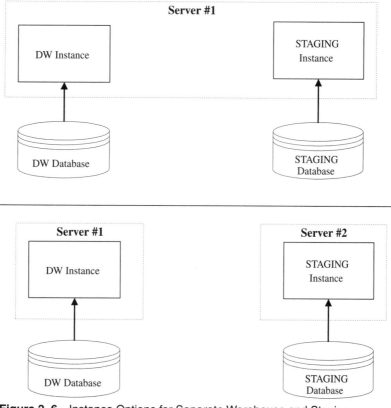

Figure 2–6   Instance Options for Separate Warehouse and Staging

- Option 1—DW and STAGING in separate databases, with multiple instances, on a single server
- Option 2—DW and STAGING in separate databases, with multiple instances, on multiple servers

Note that the first option does not make much sense unless you have a very large database server with an OS that supports partitioning of the hardware.

The first option in Figure 2–6 is similar to the second option in Figure 2–5, but it does not require the use of OPS/RAC. It too suffers from the limited shared memory allocation among multiple SGAs problem. Likewise, this method also requires proper coding and execution of the ETL code to eliminate 2PCs.

The second option in Figure 2–6 is similar to the third option in Figure 2–5, but it does not require the use of OPS/RAC. It too requires buying more than one server, which may cost more than a single server with sufficient capacity. Likewise, it too requires the network connection between the servers to be ultra-high–speed, and preferably dedicated.

RECOMMENDED ORACLE ARCHITECTURE

With all these various architectural design options, it should be evident that the software architecture is the single most important determinant of success. As stated earlier, the end-users' business intelligence software selection and/or general user interface preferences will often decide the need for application and/or Web servers. So, the data warehousing DBA can concentrate on the database server architecture. In short, the data warehousing DBA must decide on two basic issues: number and method. When considering the issue of number, the DBA must know how many servers, instances, and databases the data warehouse will have. And, when contemplating the issue of method, the DBA must know how the data will be loaded and then accessed. Thus, if you've read the last two sections carefully, you'll see that this is really all one and the same question. And you should be able to very easily answer that question based on your needs rather than just taking generic advice. But for those who still want to hear the advice, here we go.

Let's start by eliminating certain architectural choices that suffer from potential performance issues and excessive administrative complexities. In other words, let's stick to faster and simpler designs. With that in mind, we should be able to eliminate the following:

- Multiple database instances on one server (2PC and DBLINK performance)
- Multiple databases and multiple servers (2PC and network performance)
- The OPS/RAC option (overly complex administration and network performance)

Thus, we are left with a very simple conclusion: For an enterprise data warehouse, a setup with a single instance and database on one big server is better than multiple instances across many smaller servers accessing either distinct or shared databases. And, in many cases, a staging area makes sense and is advisable. This is a simple, yet effective and efficient choice. It also has the advantage of being the most well-known Oracle architecture, thus leveraging existing and common DBA skill sets. In other words, you don't need to hire a special or overly expensive DBA based on architectural needs.

The advice for people doing multiple data marts is nearly as simple: You should have $N+1$ databases and instances, where N is the number of data marts. The extra database and instance is for a common staging area from which to perform centralized ETL operations. Unlike the enterprise data warehouse where staging is an option, for data marts, the staging area is a necessity as there will be common information that will span data marts. Otherwise, your ETL programs will duplicate work. As for the servers, you should either place those instances on one large server (possibly partitioned) or across several smaller servers based on each data mart's transactional needs.

The more important point is how we arrived at these conclusions. We did not subscribe to any hardware or software vendor's recommendations. We instead concentrated on answering some very basic software architectural questions related to how we wanted to construct a data warehousing application. With this logically based information in hand, it became much simpler to select the appropriate hardware and software for a successful data warehouse.

GREAT OPERATING SYSTEM DEBATE

No discussion on software architecture would be complete without the mandatory argument over operating systems. System administrators and Oracle DBAs love to debate over which OS is ultimately better: UNIX or Windows NT/2000/XP. In fact, Democrats and Republicans often agree on more issues than UNIX and Windows bigots. Likewise, the Microsoft SQL Server versus Oracle debate is equally as heated. Be that as it may, there exists a relatively simple guideline for such selections: Let the size of the data warehouse be the deciding factor (see Table 2–1).

Table 2–1   Platform Recommendations Based Upon Database Size

	INTEL				RISC		
	NT/2000/XP		Linux		NT		UNIX/Linux
GB	SQL Server	Oracle	Oracle	SQL Server		Oracle	Oracle
10's	✔	✔	✔	✔		✔	✔
100's	✘	✔	✔	✘		✔	✔
1000's	✘	✘	✘	✘		✘	✔

Without trying to evoke a huge argument, let me explain. Mid- to large-scale RISC-based UNIX/Linux platforms are currently much more scaleable than their Intel counterparts running either Windows or Linux. For example, Sun servers can hold up to 106 CPUs, while Intel-based solutions currently max out at 8. Plus, Sun servers can hold up to 60 GB of RAM, while Intel-based solutions max out at around 16. Of course, joint development ventures such as IA-64 between HP and Intel will only serve to blur these lines further, as the IA-64 architecture is expected to scale out to 2048 processors and run NT, Linux, HP-UX, AIX, and others.

The one possible Intel-based architecture that might work is Linux and OPS/RAC to build a multi-node, multi-CPU processing behemoth—a PC-based supercomputer of sorts. But this technology is still relatively new, so it is not something I can recommend based on detailed experience.

For now, very large data warehouses should be on Oracle 8i or 9i running on RISC-based UNIX/Linux.

THE GREAT PROGRAMMING LANGUAGE DEBATE

Another explosive topic is what programming language to use for writing the ETL processes. The choices are somewhat limited as Oracle only offers PL/SQL, Java, and 3-GL pre-compilers for Ada, C, COBOL, FORTRAN, and Pascal. Oracle also offers loading utilities such as SQL Loader, which has a control language. Additionally, people use scripting languages such as Perl and Python to access Oracle databases. And of course, there are numerous third-party vendor tools as well. All have something to offer.

The key point is to select whatever language most of your developers are comfortable with. The runtime differences for loading data via PL/SQL versus Pro-C versus SQL Loader are much more a factor of your developers' comfort level and programming techniques than the speed of the underlying language. For example, an infinite loop in C does not finish any quicker than one written in PL/SQL.

THE SERIAL VS. PARALLEL PROGRAMMING DEBATE

The final software architectural issue concerns ETL program execution models. Will the data loading processes be done serially or in parallel? This is probably one of the most overlooked architectural issues in data warehousing.

It's been over 10 years since I've worked on a uniprocessor database server. The typical database server generally has four to six CPUs, and the typical data warehouse server even more. So the question of serial versus parallel program design is warranted.

In reality, the loading program's design is the key factor for the fastest possible data loads into any large-scale data warehouse. Data loading programs must be designed to utilize SMP/MPP architectures, otherwise CPU usage may not exceed 1/No. of CPUs. The Golden Rules are very simple:

- Minimize inter-process wait states.
- Maximize total concurrent CPU usage.

For example, suppose you have a file with 1000 records and each must pass though Process A and then Process B. Each process takes one unit of time to process a record. If the program design is purely serial, as in Figure 2–7, then the total runtime is roughly 2000 units of time. The problem is that Process B cannot start until after Process A has completed. Unfortunately, this is the way most programmers write code.

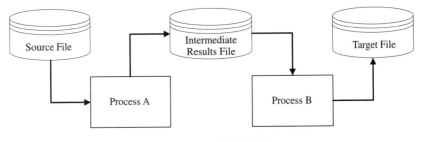

Figure 2–7   Serial ETL Processing with Wait States

To eliminate the inter-process wait time, we can replace the temporary file with a pipe. Pipes are supported by most operating systems, including UNIX/Linux and NT. The program design now looks like Figure 2–8, with a total runtime of roughly 1001 units (there is a one-unit time lag for the very first record to be completely processed through the pipe). This represents a nearly 100% improvement over the original serial solution.

To maximize CPU usage, we can fork multiple A/B process pairs to divide and conquer the 1000 records. Each process pair would handle $1/N$ records, where N is the number of CPUs. If we assume four CPUs, then the picture would look like Figure 2–9, with a total runtime of roughly 251 units (there is a one-unit time lag for the very first record to be completely processed through the pipe). This represents a nearly 700% improvement over the original serial solution. This technique should be the standard for most data warehouse programming efforts.

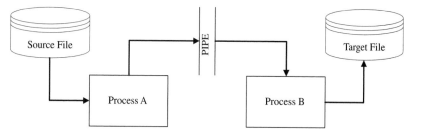

Figure 2–8   Basic Parallel ETL Processing via Pipes

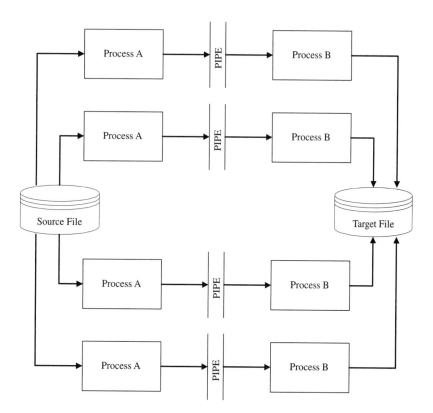

Figure 2–9   True Parallel EFL Processing via Forking

Let me give you a real-world example of just how big a difference this kind of software architectural issue can make. And don't laugh at how silly this example sounds. It really happened this way on my 7-Eleven data warehouse.

We had a nightly batch window of about eight hours to run all our data warehouse ETL jobs. At some point, just one of our jobs started to take 4.5 hours to run, so we could no longer complete our load cycle within the time allowed. At the time, our hardware included:

- 8 400MHz 64-bit CPUs
- 4 GB RAM
- 2 GB EMC cache
- RAID-5

Rather than listen to the DBA and effect a software redesign, management decided to upgrade the hardware. They felt that this would provide an immediate and measurable payback. Plus, it was very easy to manage—one down weekend to install all the upgrades. And they sold the customer on it. So we upgraded to:

- 16 400MHz 64-bit CPUs
- 8 GB RAM
- 4 GB EMC cache (this was the most expensive item)
- RAID 0+1 (faster writes at cost of doubling the number of disks)

All that hardware cost nearly a million dollars, and all we got was a 15-minute improvement! In the long term, our data warehouse was scaling up in terms of concurrent users and queries per day, so the money really was not wasted. We merely ended up ordering some necessary hardware upgrades a few months earlier than necessary or planned.

After that fiasco, management authorized me to redesign the ETL process. So, I merely applied the Golden Rules: Minimize inter-process wait states and maximize total concurrent CPU usage. I first converted the existing program to "divide and conquer" the input data into 16 concurrent streams, with each stream feeding an instantiation of the program. I modified the job to not wait for any step to complete before starting a subsequent step.

In terms of hours, this was a dirt-cheap fix. The time spent was merely 30 minutes for some simple UNIX shell scripting changes and a few hours of time to modify the program and job schedule. The result was a total runtime of 20 minutes. Finally, I made one last tuning modification using Dynamic SQL Method 2: prepare and execute. The result was a total runtime of 15 minutes. We estimated the costs in terms of time at $2600, yielding 17 times the throughput at 385 times less than the costs of the hardware upgrades! I got my bonus that quarter.

Hardware Architecture

With the software architecture properly defined, the next biggest challenge for the data warehouse DBA is to select an appropriate hardware platform for implementation.

In theory, data warehouse hardware selection should be simple. Data warehouses are huge, so common sense would dictate ordering large, scalable systems. Once you start throwing around the "T" word (for terabytes) when referring to your data warehouse, then lots of CPUs and lots of disks should not be a hard sell. If you need further convincing, then reexamine your data warehouse's mission statement and sponsor. A data warehouse enabling both executives and senior management to form strategic business decisions is worth a lot to any business. Hence, you would fully expect a hardware budget in line with that supposition. In short, data warehouse platforms are not cheap.

As simple as I've tried to make the hardware budget and selection process sound, nothing in life works as simply as we think it should. It's not unusual for many mid- to large-sized companies to have preferred hardware and software vendors who typically have early and direct access to project requirements. Furthermore, such vendors often provide streamlined ordering, price breaks, and other perks to attract and maintain key accounts. As such, it often occurs that hardware decisions have already been made by the time the DBA becomes involved with the data warehouse. Don't let this happen, because even the best software architecture will fail on the wrong hardware.

Another challenge with hardware selection is the rapid pace of technological advancement. Even the people selling the hardware have a tough time keeping up with just their company's offerings. The poor DBA often must serve as an expert across the various hardware vendors and their offerings, such as servers, disk arrays, tape management systems, etc. Add to that all the related software and it's no wonder that this phase can leave many DBAs stressed and second-guessing. Of course, between the vendors, business sponsor, technical management, developers, DBAs, and system administrators, there will be no shortage of well-intended advice.

The final challenge is to pick a platform that has a committed growth path from the vendor. With IA-64 and other new technologies, some RISC architectures may not have a simple and straightforward growth path. There may be cabinet, board, or bus swap-outs, and possibly even OS switches required. Press the vendors extremely hard on this issue because whatever hardware you buy must be scalable both in terms of database size and concurrent users.

If as the DBA you are lucky enough to be involved from the start, review all the technological offerings and find a hardware platform with a well-defined growth path—it's safe to bet that it will be the hardware vendor's premier equipment. No one said that a data warehouse would be cheap! If the budget is tight, do not compromise on lesser equipment. The cost to replace the wrong hardware selection is generally more than that of the delay to secure additional initial budget. Remember, a data warehouse can be delayed. It is not a core business system like OLTP and ERP applications (i.e., a business can go on without a data warehouse), so wait for sufficient funding.

FOUR BASIC QUESTIONS

Selecting hardware can be as simple as answering four basic hardware architecture questions:

- How many CPUs?
- How much memory?

- How much disk space?
- What disk configuration?

While this may seem like a gross oversimplification, the CPU count alone is generally sufficient to select among the pertinent hardware architectures available.

How Many CPUs?

The first major hardware question is: How many CPUs? This relatively simple question actually has two parts. First, what's the expected maximum number of concurrent queries? This is a much more involved question than just determining the number of reporting users who might access the data warehouse. The suggested procedure is to calculate the maximum number of concurrent users times the maximum number of concurrent reports per user that the end-user business intelligence tool permits. Plus, remember earlier we said that typical business intelligence tools often submit dozens of queries per report execution, some of whose execution may be submitted in parallel. So, the actual number of Oracle connections submitting queries could be as high as:

Concurrent Users * Concurrent Reports per User * Concurrent Queries Spawned per Report Execution

Let's assume that we'll have 25 concurrent users and that each user may submit up to 10 concurrent reports execution requests. Furthermore, let's assume that although our business intelligence tool typically generates about five SQL query statements per report, it nonetheless submits no more than four SQL query statements concurrently. This yields 1000 potential concurrent Oracle query processes!

Second, what degree of parallelism will the average query utilize (if any)? Oracle's Parallel Query Option (PQO) permits Oracle to spawn (i.e., fork) multiple processes to handle a given query. It is a true "divide and conquer" technique to improve query response time.

Returning to our simple example, let's further assume that the DBA has the warehouse tables set up for parallel query with a degree of four. This takes our total potential concurrent Oracle query process count to 4000! That's potentially 4000 concurrent query processes to support just 25 business intelligence users.

I did not define this example to sound so outrageous. But it does hopefully make it clear that the Oracle parallel degree setting requires much more thought than just looking at how many CPUs there are on the data warehouse's server. I've seen several data warehousing projects with 32–64 CPUs and a parallel degree setting equal to the CPU count—and these systems are performing like dogs. Once I ask them how many concurrent users they have and inquire about their business intelligence tool's process architecture, I find that either or both the concurrent user count and concurrent query process count are greater than the number of CPUs. We then generally correct their performance problem by merely reducing the parallel degree— sometimes all the way back down to one (i.e., serial). I see this problem all the time, especially on smaller servers with just 4–16 CPUs.

So the logical question at this point is: Is there some way to quantify this need? If we assume that the effective throughput per CPU is roughly eight times that of the disk subsystem (i.e., one CPU can generally saturate eight cached disks) and that we must have at least four CPUs in a data warehouse, we arrive at the following equation:

No. of CPUs = Max (Concurrent Users * Avg. Concurrent Queries per User * PQO Degree/8, 4)

The results are shown in Figure 3–1.

So what does this graph show us? Well, even for parallel degree one (i.e., serial query processing), we need to double our CPU count at 64 concurrent queries and double it yet again at 128 concurrent queries. Remembering our earlier comments about business intelligence users, their concurrent reports, and concurrent queries per report, 128 queries could well be just one business intelligence user!

Hopefully, the results in Figure 3–1 make it painfully clear that scalable, multi-processor hardware is truly required. Most data warehouses will have lots of concurrent users and queries, plus utilize PQO, so a hardware platform that that can scale up to 32 processors is a genuine minimum requirement—and the ability to scale to 64 or more CPUs is a definite plus. An overview of available parallel architectures is shown in Table 3–1.

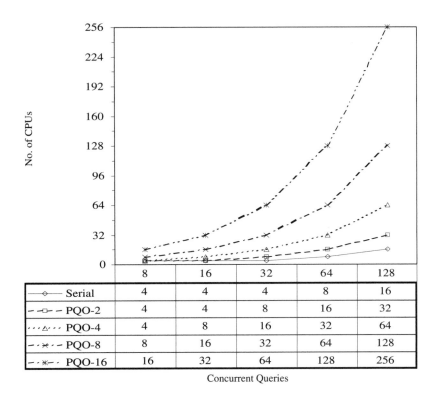

Figure 3–1   Example Parallel Query CPU Usage

Table 3–1   Common Parallel Hardware Architectures

Architecture	CPU Limit	Shared Memory	Shared Disks	OS Instances	PQO	OPS
SMP	32	Yes	Yes	1	Preferred	Unnecessary
SMP + Crossbar	106	Yes	Yes	1	Preferred	Unnecessary
NUMA	64	Yes	Yes	1	Preferred	Unnecessary
Cluster	1024	No	Yes	No. of Nodes	Preferred	Preferred
MPP	4096	No	No	No. of CPUs	Required	Required

The first architecture to consider is SMP, shown in Figure 3–2. SMP is essentially a uniprocessor architecture with multiple CPUs, all sharing memory and disk. The advantages of SMP include:

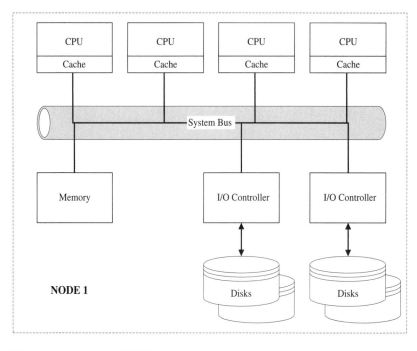

Figure 3–2   Typical SMP Hardware Architecture

- Proven, reliable technology (has been around for years)
- Wide vendor selection (most offer SMP servers)
- Easy to set up, manage, and upgrade (single OS)
- Excellent performance within scalability range
- No special programming methods or tools required

The primary disadvantage is that SMP servers are generally limited to 32 processors. This limitation eliminates SMP servers as a solution for highly concurrent and parallel data warehouse implementations (i.e., the bottom right corner of Table 3–1). The reason is that SMP servers saturate the system bus as they increase the number of CPUs. The SMP server must maintain inter-CPU cache consistency plus perform all memory, disk, and peripheral operations over a single high-speed system bus. Moreover, system bus length versus speed limitation comes into play.

This does not mean that SMP servers are a bad choice. If you know your needs or budget will not exceed 32 CPUs, SMP is a great choice. SMP is like the perfect work car: common, inexpensive, reliable, economical, and fast—all at the same time.

The second architecture to consider is SMP with a crossbar that interconnects topologies. In this architecture, every board is directly connected to every other board. Hence, no interconnect requests have to share the same bus as with traditional SMP machines. Thus, these boxes can scale to more CPUs while at the same time maintaining a uniform memory access time. In essence, such machines are really second-generation SMP machines. You get all the benefits of SMP plus more CPUs. These platforms are a great choice.

The third architecture to consider is the non-uniform memory access (NUMA) architecture shown in Figure 3–3. Here nodes have one or more local processor groups connected via a high-speed interconnect, and each processor group implements a portion of the single memory address space and common disk pool. The key advantages of the NUMA architecture include:

- Reliability similar to SMP architecture
- More scalable than SMP architecture
- Easy to set up, manage, and upgrade (single OS)
- Performance approaching SMP architecture
- No special programming methods or tools required

NUMA servers have few disadvantages. There are only a few vendors offering NUMA. The CPU count must be increased in increments of the group size, typically four. Current NUMA machines generally top out at 64 CPUs (i.e., 16 groups of 4). Also note that some vendors provide external interconnect devices to link multiple SMP boxes into a pseudo-NUMA architecture machine, validating that NUMA is basically a better SMP than SMP.

The fourth architecture to consider is clustering uniprocessor, SMP, or NUMA machines. Figure 3–4 demonstrates two clustered SMP machines. A cluster is essentially a loosely coupled network of autonomous nodes, each with its own CPU, memory, and OS, but with specialized hardware to provide a common pool of disks to all nodes in the system. The advantages of clustering include:

- Proven technology (introduced mid-1980s by DEC with VAX VMS clusters)

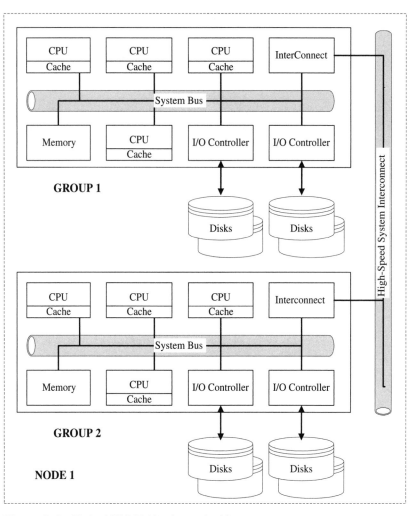

Figure 3–3 Typical NUMA Hardware Architecture

- Wide vendor selection (many offer clustering for their SMP or NUMA servers)
- High availability, or HA (eliminates any individual node as a single point of failure)

However, there are some drawbacks:

- Requires OPS to utilize all resources
- Less reliable due to hardware and software coordination issues

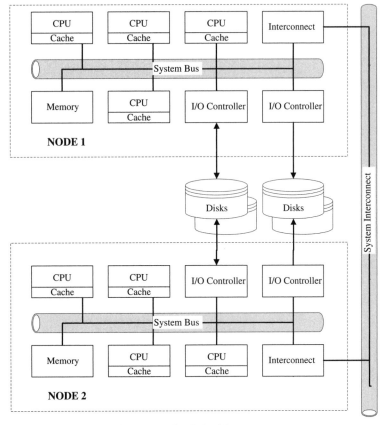

Figure 3–4 Typical Clustered SMP Architecture

- Difficult to set up, manage, and upgrade (multiple OS and OPS instances)
- Poor performance scalability due to multiple operating systems, OPS, and shared disk overheads
- Long database startups and recoveries as only one node can do instance recovery

Nonetheless, clustering SMP and NUMA machines is quite popular.

A final architecture to consider is MPP, shown in Figure 3–5. MPP is essentially a very tightly coupled network of autonomous nodes, each with its own CPU, memory, disk, and OS, and with software to make all the disks available to every node in the system. The

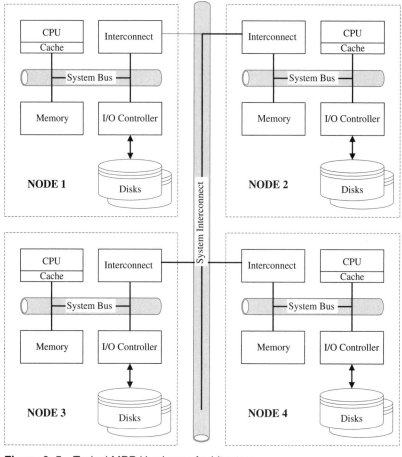

Figure 3–5   Typical MPP Hardware Architecture

primary advantage is that MPP servers generally scale higher than any other parallel architecture, with configurations as high as 4096 CPUs.

But, MPP servers have many disadvantages, including:

•   Require OPS to utilize all resources
•   Less reliable due to hardware and software coordination issues
•   Narrower vendor selection (few offer MPP servers)
•   Hard to set up, manage, and upgrade (multiple OS and OPS instances)

- Poor performance scalability due to multiple operating systems, OPS, and shared disk overheads
- Complex database design for reducing interconnect data traffic utilizing disk affinity
- Long database startups and recoveries as only one node can do instance recovery

HOW MUCH MEMORY?

The second major hardware question is: How much memory? Fortunately, this is very simple to answer. When in doubt, buy as much memory as your budget can afford and your server can accommodate. No other hardware component as generally, easily, or quickly provides such dynamic performance improvements. Moreover, memory is by far the easiest hardware component to incrementally augment as time goes on. If you don't get enough memory at the start, don't hesitate to add more. Just make sure that you adjust your database and application parameters to take full advantage of all memory.

So, do you just order as much memory as the server can hold or the budget can afford? What if you have multiple servers? Fortunately, you can be a bit more scientific with your estimates. In fact, you can use the same criteria from the CPU needs analysis to derive a more meaningful memory need estimate.

If we assume Oracle consumes about 50 MB of memory per business intelligence query process, (based in large part upon proper INIT.ORA parameter settings, covered in Chapter 5), and that we must have at least 1 GB of RAM, we arrive at the following formula:

GB RAM = Round (Max (Concurrent Users * Avg. Concurrent Queries per User * PQO Degree * 50, 1000)/1000,0)

The results are shown in Figure 3–6.

Keep in mind that you'll need to equally spread all that memory across whatever number of nodes you end up with. Also remember that most SMP and NUMA machines can have up to 64 GB of RAM, so they can address the needs for all but the largest of data warehouses (i.e., bottom right corner cell of Figure 3–6).

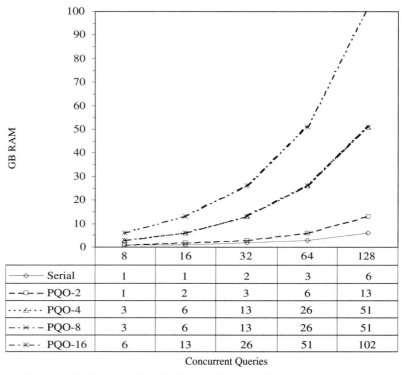

	8	16	32	64	128
⎯◇⎯ Serial	1	1	2	3	6
− −□− − PQO-2	1	2	3	6	13
· · ·△· · · PQO-4	3	6	13	26	51
− · ✕ · − PQO-8	3	6	13	26	51
− · ✳− · PQO-16	6	13	26	51	102

Concurrent Queries

Figure 3–6   Example Parallel Query Memory Usage

So what does this graph show us? Well, even for parallel degree one (i.e., serial query processing), we need at least 2 GB of memory for even just a few queries. In fact, the graph suggests 6–26 GB for mid-size data warehouses, and 60+ GB (often the limit) for the largest data warehouses. And don't forget to factor in your data loading memory needs—they might be above and beyond what this graph suggests.

HOW MANY OF WHAT DISKS?

The third and fourth major hardware questions are:

• How much disk space?
• What disk configuration?

These two questions should be resolved together. Gone for good are the days of just buying SCSI controllers and disks for servers. Today's data warehouses are far too big for that kind of solution—they must be built using disk arrays.

A disk array is a cabinet that houses front-end and back-end intelligent controllers, a sizable memory cache, and a very large disk farm (Figure 3–7). There are two kinds of disk arrays:

- SAN
- NAS

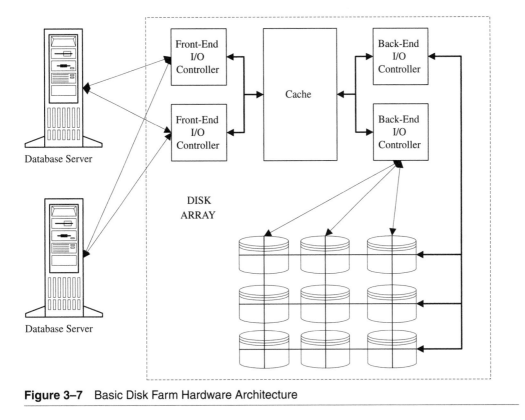

Figure 3–7 Basic Disk Farm Hardware Architecture

A SAN is a disk farm appliance. It's a shared, dedicated, high-speed network connecting servers and disks, typically via fiber channel. I've heard SAN referred to as "simply a bunch of disks strung together with a bit of fiber optics." The underlying technology is SCSI.

A NAS is a disk farm on a network. It's a special-purpose server with its own embedded software for file sharing across the network. I've heard NAS referred to as "just a RAID array with an Ethernet card." The underlying technology is network file system (NFS).

There are great debates between both camps on whether SAN or NAS is better. I don't subscribe to these arguments for I've used both technologies without incident on large data warehouses. I can say that given a choice, I've found SAN to offer better performance with the large block sizes, high throughput, and write-intensive nature of large data warehouses. I also prefer NAS's centralized manageability and configuration flexibility. But, these differences are blurring as the lines between these two technologies continue to fade.

Probably the best-known SAN disk arrays are from EMC Corporation. But vendors such as Sun, HP, Compaq, and IBM have offerings as well. Be forewarned that disk arrays are quite expensive. It's not uncommon for a disk array to cost as much or more than a database server. Often this high cost is in direct proportion to the cache size as disk arrays use very expensive high-speed memory. But, since the disk drives in them are often nothing more than next-generation PC server SCSI drives, the cache memory size is critical for obtaining acceptable performance. It's recommended that for big data warehouses, the disk array's cache be anywhere from 2–8 GB.

When selecting a disk array, make sure that it is scalable along four criteria. First, it must provide enough front-end controllers for the number of servers you may need to connect. Second, it must offer an initial and maximum cache memory size that will handle your maximum expected I/O needs while maintaining a 40% or better cache hit ratio. Third, it must provide sufficient bays for the number and size of disk drives that you desire to use. And finally, the disk array should be able to interconnect with other disk arrays from the same manufacturer or other vendors. It may sound funny, but with today's relatively cheap disk space costs, data warehouses are growing to multi-terabyte sizes and beyond. Often, it will take more than one disk array cabinet to hold that much data.

If all that were not enough, most disk arrays support RAID, so you need to choose a RAID level to employ. The typical choices are RAID 0, 1, 0+1, and 3–5, where:

- RAID 0 non-redundantly stripes data across multiple drives for speed.
- RAID 1 mirrors data across multiple disks for 100% data redundancy.
- RAID 0+1 combines RAID 0 and RAID 1 for speed and data protection.
- RAID 3 stripes bytes across multiple drives with a dedicated parity disk.
- RAID 4 stripes blocks across multiple drives with a dedicated parity disk.
- RAID 5 stripes both blocks and parity information across multiple drives.

In summary, the various RAID levels with their pros and cons are shown in Table 3–2.

Table 3–2   Comparison of RAID Levels

RAID Level	Min No. of Drives	Redundancy	Striping	Read	Write
0	2	None	Block	Fast	Fast
1	2	Best	None	Fast	Fast
0+1	4	Best	Block	Fast	Fast
3	3	Good	Byte	Fast	Slow
4	3	Good	Block	Fast	Slow
5	3	Better	Block	Fast	Slow

Another way to view this is that for high write rates (i.e., redo logs, rollback segments, and temporary segments), RAID 0+1 is the best possible HA solution. RAID 5's writes are just too expensive at 3–4 times those of RAID 0. And for high read rates (i.e., read-only tablespaces and other segments used during query-only usage), RAID 5 is the best HA solution. RAID 0+1 is just too expensive per GB; it is two times that of RAID 0.

Since most users desire an HA data warehouse solution, the only valid choices are RAID 0+1 and RAID 5. The data warehousing DBA will have to decide whether disk space or loading time is in shorter supply. Assuming that a data warehouse will require 1.5 terabytes of usable disk space, Table 3–3 shows just how many disks are needed for typical RAID 0+1 and RAID 5 solutions.

Table 3–3   Example of RAID Selection vs. Usable Disk Space

RAID Level	Usable GB	Actual GB	18GB Drives	36GB Drives
0+1	1500	3000	167	84
5	1500	1875	105	53

The key issue is the physical number of drives required. Disk array vendors sell different cabinet and cache sizes based on the physical number of drives to be housed. Obviously, the bigger cabinets and caches that handle larger disk farms cost more money. You can also use multiple disk arrays, assuming that you prefer more, smaller drives instead of 18GB or 36GB drives. The RAID 0+1 solution would then consume 334 9GB drives. There are few, if any disk array cabinets that size, so you'd have to buy multiple disk arrays. That sounds easy, but remember that would require buying very expensive high-speed memory for each disk array. Moreover, it would require splitting your database server's I/O channels across those disk arrays, thereby reducing your overall I/O bandwidth per database server (i.e., each database server has: *No. of Controllers/No. of Disk Arrays in Bandwidth per Disk Array*).

There's one final and key aspect to successfully implementing RAID 0+1 and RAID 5 disk configurations: choosing the optimal stripe size and stripe set size. This is probably the least understood and most debated aspect of RAID for data warehousing. Striping is simply the process of writing data across multiple disk drives to maximize the number of drives handling each I/O request. It's another "divide and conquer" technique. The idea is that N drives working together should be able to complete an I/O request quicker than one drive. The stripe size is the number of bytes written to a disk before switching to the next disk in the same group, and the stripe set is the number of disks from that group.

Figure 3–8 shows an example of RAID 0+1 with a stripe size of 64 kilobytes (K) and a stripe set size of 4. That means that four disks form a group where every 64K is on a different disk. Bytes 1–64 are on Disk 1, Bytes 65–128 are on Disk 2, and so on. If an I/O request is larger than 256K (i.e., *Stripe Size * Stripe Set Size*), then that I/O request wraps back around to Disk 1 and repeats the entire process, which can be a performance problem. Look again at Figure 3–8 and assume we need to write 512K to a table whose Oracle data blocks all are within the same data file. We'll be asking the disk array to perform eight concurrent 64K writes to the same stripe set, or two 64K writes per physical disk. We would have been much better off if the stripe set size had been eight drives or if the data had been spread across two data files that fell into two different stripe sets, so that eight different physical disk drives could have handled the eight concurrent write requests.

MIRROR 1

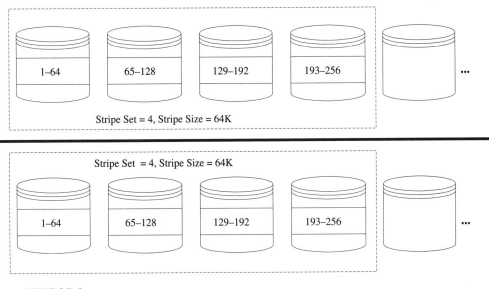

MIRROR 2

Figure 3–8   Example RAID 0+1 Striping Parameters

Translation: The data warehousing DBA must very carefully consider the database block size and multi-block initialization parameter settings when choosing the stripe size and stripe set size. RAID I/O performance can be improved or set back an order of magnitude by the positive or negative interaction of these settings.

RECOMMENDED HARDWARE ARCHITECTURE

Even with the plethora of hardware choices introduced in the previous sections, picking your data warehousing hardware is actually quite easy. Typical needs include:

- Scalable, multi-processor server platform
- Sufficient memory for parallel processing
- Highly scalable disk storage system
- Sufficient disk cache for > 50% hit ratio
- Striping for better I/O performance
- Data redundancy for data protection
- Support for both fast reads and writes

Combined with our proposed software architecture requirements for:

- Single server
- Single instance
- Single database
- Oracle 8i or 9i
- RISC-based UNIX
- Parallel load programs

The recommended minimum data warehousing hardware platform is:

- SMP or NUMA server
- 8–16 64-bit RISC CPUs
- True 64-bit UNIX OS
- 4–8 GB RAM
- Mid- to large-sized disk array
- 2–4 GB disk cache
- RAID 0+1 via hardware
- 18GB or 36GB disk drives

Again, let me stress that this is not based on any anti-NT sentiments or UNIX bigotry. From my experience loading and querying terabytes of data, I've found data warehouses generally consume CPU and I/O bandwidth far beyond the capacity of Intel-based SMP servers and Windows NT/2000, even when clustered. The only Intel-based solutions that seriously qualify for a data warehouse implementation are IBM's (a.k.a. Sequent's) NUMA-Q machine with 64 Pentium III Xeons or IA-64s running DYNIX/ptx or a Data General Aviion AV2500 with 64 Pentium III Xeons running DG/UX. Even though both these machines could run Windows NT/2000, they would not be able to scale to the same CPU count as under their respective UNIX OS.

Examples of acceptable SMP and NUMA servers from first-tier vendors are shown in Table 3–4.

Table 3–4   Example SMP and NUMA Hardware Platforms

Vendor	Server Family	OS	Cluster Software	CPUs
Compaq	AlphaServer	Tru64 UNIX	TruCluster Server	Alpha
Data General	Aviion	DG/UX	DG/UX Clusters	Xeon / IA-64
HP	9000 V-Class	HP/UX	MC/ServiceGuard	PA-RISC / IA-64
IBM	RS/6000	AIX	HACMP	PowerPC RS64 III
IBM (Sequent)	NUMA-Q	DYNIX/ptx	ptx/CLUSTERS	Xeon / IA-64
Silicon Graphics	SGI 2000	IRIX	IRIS FailSafe	MIPS RISC R12000
Sun	E Line	Solaris	Sun Clusters	UltraSPARC

Examples of acceptable disk arrays from first-tier vendors are shown in Table 3–5.

Table 3–5   Example Disk Array Offerings from Vendors

Vendor	Array Family	Max Cache GB	Max Drive GB	Max Terabytes
Compaq	Modular Array	3	36	2.6
EMC	Symmetrix	32	50	19.1
HP	SureStore	16	47	11.0
IBM	Storage Server	16	36	11.2
Sun	StorEdge T3	8.5	36	88.0

The stripe size and stripe set size are both a bit too subjective for any universal recommendations. In general, choose a stripe size 4–8 times your Oracle block size and a stripe set size of 4–8 disks. So, for a 16K Oracle block size, a stripe size of 128K and a stripe set size of 8 should work well for 1MB I/O requests. Of course, the following Oracle initialization parameters would have to be set to 64 to guarantee optimal striping performance:

- DB_FILE_MULTIBLOCK_READ_COUNT
- SORT_MULTIBLOCK_READ_COUNT
- HASH_MULTIBLOCK_IO_COUNT
- DB_FILE_DIRECT_IO_COUNT

THE GREAT VENDOR DEBATE

When once asked about his best play, Willie Mays said, "I don't compare 'em, I just catch 'em." I feel the same way about hardware vendors; they just sell computers. But for many people, discussions comparing vendors can quickly get ugly. You'd think these people worked for or had huge stock holdings in their vendor of choice. More often than not, it's just an issue of comfort. If you've been a DBA for the past five years on platform X, then you'll often argue why it's the best platform out there, regardless of reality. We all do it; it's just human nature.

Nonetheless, there is a very clear hardware vendor that is, arguably, the best choice for building an Oracle data warehouse, and that's Sun. Let me explain.

First, Sun easily meets the basic hardware requirements. Sun's Enterprise 10000 is an SMP machine that scales to 64 processors. Moreover, the HPC 10000 can be clustered to 1024 processors. Plus, Solaris is a fairly robust and proven 64-bit version of the UNIX OS. And let's not forget the UltraSPARC, Sun's latest generation of the proven and potent SPARC CPU architecture.

Second, there are plenty of DBAs, developers, and system administrators familiar with Sun and Solaris. So, staffing the data warehouse project will be easy. From my experience, many DBAs and developers have worked on all the big three UNIX versions: Solaris, AIX, and HP-

UX (and increasingly now, Linux). So, Sun and Solaris should not surprise or offend the critical masses.

The main reason to pick Sun is that's where Oracle develops, so new versions and patches come out on Solaris first. In OLTP environments, DBAs tend to wait six months after a patch is released before installing it. That's fine for OLTP database needs, but data warehouses are different. Data warehouses are huge, with tables in the hundreds of millions or billions of rows. You will experience lots of Oracle problems with databases this size. Whether it is parallel query process failures, incorrect explain plans for partition eliminations, or corrupted bitmap indexes, count on encountering lots of Oracle problems and needing patches as quickly as possible.

Just as a point of reference: I did my last data warehouse on an HP server. I also do not own any shares of Sun stock. So, I honestly do not feel like I am making this recommendation based on any personal prejudices.

THE 32- VS. 64-BIT ORACLE DEBATE

Another issue that gets a lot of attention is whether you should run 32-bit or 64-bit Oracle on your 64-bit UNIX. At first this sounds like a dumb question, right? But for some of the platforms, the answer may very well surprise you. For example, Oracle's Metalink technical support site quotes that:

- 32-bit Oracle on HP-UX 11.00 32-bit—No difference
- 32-bit Oracle on HP-UX 11.00 64-bit—1–2% degradation
- 64-bit Oracle on HP-UX 11.00 64-bit—8–9% degradation

And here I thought that 64-bit was always faster. The point is: Know your target platform and its Oracle ports. Don't just assume that bigger is better.

Then there's the ever-popular question of the maximum system-wide SGA size limit of 32-bit versus 64-bit Oracle. For example, with 32-bit Oracle, the maximum system-wide SGA size limit is 1.75 GB for HP-UX (or, when using memory windows, 1 GB per instance with another .75 shared system-wide) and 3.75 GB for Solaris. But with either of these operating systems running the 64-bit version of

Oracle, the maximum system-wide SGA size is limited only by the physical amount of memory present on the machine.

Finally, there's the new version and patch issue again. Oracle historically released the 32-bit versions first. But now, Oracle seems fully committed to doing the 64-bit versions first, with some platforms no longer even offering 32-bit versions. Again, you need to know your target platform and its Oracle ports.

If you've accepted the prior recommendation for Sun hardware, there is a clear answer: 64-bit Oracle all the way. On Sun Solaris, 64-bit Oracle is faster than the 32-bit version—you'll need those very large SGAs for good I/O performance—and remember, new releases and patches come out on Sun first. Plus, 64-bit on Sun is the only version now supported.

THE RAW VS. COOKED FILES DEBATE

Another question that often arises is whether to use raw or cooked files. The answer here is very simple: Use cooked files. The only time to use raw files is for OPS as it is a key requirement.

Raw files offer two performance improvements: asynchronous I/O and no double-caching (i.e., caching of data in Oracle SGA and UNIX file system cache). Quite often, the realized performance gain is relatively small. Some sources say 5–10%, while others wildly claim 50%. There really is no universal consensus on what the real performance gains are for using raw files. However, nearly everyone agrees that raw generally requires more skilled and well-trained administrative staff because none of the standard UNIX file system commands and many backup/recovery suites do not function with raw files. Thus, the administrative headaches alone are reason enough to avoid raw files like the plague.

Again, if you've accepted the prior recommendation for Sun hardware, then there is a clear answer: Use cooked files. Solaris supports asynchronous I/O to both raw and file system data files. The only real penalty is double-caching of data.

If you genuinely believe that you need the performance gain raw files supposedly offer, then I strongly suggest looking at the Veritas file system with its Quick IO feature. Quick IO supports asynchronous I/O and eliminates double-caching. In short, Oracle accesses database files as if they were raw even though the DBA manages them as if they were regular files. Essentially, Quick IO provides a character-mode device driver and a file system namespace mechanism. For more information, I suggest reading the white paper titled "Veritas Quick IO: Equivalent to raw volumes, yet easier." It can be found on Veritas' Web site (*www.veritas.com*, under *white papers*).

The Veritas file system also supports online file system backups, which can be used to perform online incremental database backups. Furthermore, Veritas' online incremental backup is vastly superior to using Oracle's RMAN. The key difference is that Oracle's RMAN must scan all the blocks during an online incremental database backup to see which blocks have changed. RMAN saves magnetic tapes at the expense of time. The Veritas online incremental database backup knows which blocks have changed via its file system redo logs, so it saves both tape space and time. Finally, Veritas offers one of the easiest to manage UNIX file systems and backup/recovery suites available. Unfortunately, Veritas is only available for Solaris and HP-UX.

As another point of reference, I did my last data warehouse using raw files. I also do not own any shares of Veritas stock. And, I honestly do not feel like I am making this recommendation based on any personal prejudices.

THE NEED FOR LOGICAL VOLUME MANAGERS

There are two ways to implement RAID within disk arrays. Hardware, or controller-based, RAID is implemented via firmware in the disk array. Software, or host-based, RAID is implemented via software on the host server. Of course, you can combine the two methods as well.

While it may seem that RAID via hardware would be preferable, there are some drawbacks. Often this approach requires a one-time, static configuration. If the DBA guesses wrong or if the application I/O patterns change over time, the only solution is to back up the data, reconfigure the array, and reload the data. For a multi-terabyte data warehouse, this exercise could take an entire weekend! Another issue is that different RAID configurations often cannot be mixed and matched on the same disk drive (i.e., either RAID 0+1 or RAID 5, but not both on a given disk drive). Finally, many controller-based RAID solutions offer limited tools to trace I/O patterns and gather the statistics necessary to analyze them to plan for successful reconfigurations.

Although software-based RAID will require host CPU cycles and increased I/O bus traffic, the advantages are very compelling. Host-based RAID offers just plain superior flexibility in terms of configuration. The process is not one-time, but ongoing, and it does not require backups and reloads to make changes. You also can freely mix and match RAID configurations on entire disk drives or portions of drives. For example, you could create RAID0+1 space for loading current data and RAID 5 space for loading non-current (i.e., read-only) data, with each configuration spread equally across all disk drives. Plus, software RAID generally offers very useful tools for monitoring and tuning disk space configurations. And, some vendors offer automated tools for finding and removing hot spots.

While most UNIX vendors provide a free logical volume manager (LVM) with the OS, you get what you pay for. I highly recommend a third-party vendor's LVM such as Veritas' Volume Manager. If you've adopted the Veritas file system for its Quick IO feature (see prior section on raw files), then you really should consider using their LVM as well.

So just how does the combination work? Most disk arrays first split spindles (i.e., disks) into partitions, often referred to as meta- or hyper-devices. These meta-devices are then the devices that the disk array presents to the UNIX OS. For example, if we had:

- 64 47GB disk drives (3 terabytes in total)
- Hardware-based mirroring (1.5 terabytes usable)
- 6-way split of disks into 192 7.8GB meta-devices
- LVM stripe size of 64K
- LVM stripe set size of 4 meta-devices per volume group
- 12 2GB data files per volume group
- 48 total volume groups (1.15 terabytes accessible)

The picture would look something like Figure 3–9.

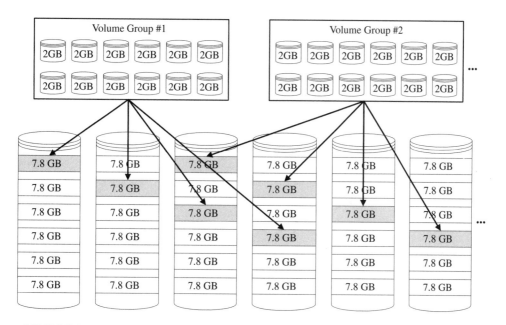

MIRROR 1

Figure 3–9   Example Logical Volume Manager Layout

Star Schema Universe

Let me start this chapter by restating this book's mission statement:

> To serve as the DBA's definitive and detailed reference regarding the successful design, construction, tuning, and maintenance of star schema data warehouses in Oracle 8i and 9i.

Note that "star schema" is much more than a term; it's a mindset. In fact, it's as big a leap in theory and technique as between hierarchical and relational databases. This mindset applies first and foremost to database design and tuning techniques. But more importantly, it directly controls which Oracle optimizer features can best be leveraged and the resulting query explain plans that can possibly be achieved.

If you're the DBA for a star schema data warehouse, then this book is for you. The techniques within are proven and not to be found elsewhere. Moreover, none of these techniques are so obvious as to be considered mainstream. To date, I've found that less than 5% of the people attending my data warehousing presentations have ever thought along the lines espoused throughout this book. Furthermore, few people seem to have read the Oracle white paper titled "Star Queries in Oracle8," published back in June of 1997 and the forefather for many of my design and tuning techniques.

Conversely, if you are the DBA for a data warehouse that is not doing star schemas, then very little in this book will be of use. While I could get back up on my soapbox from Chapter 1 regarding "What

Is a Data Warehouse?" and ask how you expect to successfully build multi-terabyte data warehouses without star schemas, it's not my intention to question or belittle your data warehouse. But I do want to set expectations properly. So once again, if you are not doing star schemas, then this book is not for you.

So let's see where star schemas came from, special challenges they pose (particularly for more experienced DBAs), what they look like, and how to successfully design them.

THE RATIONALE FOR STARS

Over the past decade, an interesting computer phenomenon has occurred: Hardware technology has grown much faster than software technology. We see this all the time in the PC market with hard drives, memory, CPUs, and video cards getting more powerful and cheaper year after year. But, the same is also true in the database server world as well. Mainstream UNIX servers and their disk storage systems have grown in similar leaps and bounds. When's the last time you managed a production Oracle database on a single-processor server? Even test and development database servers are predominately multi-processor given today's low hardware costs.

But alas, the poor Oracle database and optimizer have grown at a somewhat slower pace with regard to handling data warehouses. In fact, Oracle 8i and 9i are the first versions to truly begin tackling the monumental performance challenges posed by today's enormous data warehouses. And as I stated back in Chapter 2, "Software Architecture," you cannot successfully do multi-terabyte data warehouses in Oracle prior to Oracle 8i.

Back in the early 1990s, Ralph Kimball began proposing new relational database design techniques to make data warehouses both understandable and fast. His technique, known as dimensional modeling, makes data warehouses faster by limiting the number of join operations that the database optimizer has to handle. Since join operations are generally quite expensive and since the major database vendors have only recently significantly improved their query optimizers for such large joins, Ralph's database design techniques have become a true staple for data warehousing.

Of course, it is possible to build successful very large databases, not data warehouses, without using star schemas. But you'll find that both Oracle 8i and 9i support star schemas via database initialization parameters, object partitioning, indexing options, explain plans, and materialized views. For example, the same query ran as follows:

- Over 12 hours on Oracle 7.3
- Under 12 minutes on Oracle 8.0
- Under 8 minutes on Oracle 8i
- Under 4 minutes on Oracle 9i

The tables, indexes, and rows of data were exactly the same; only the database initialization parameters (chosen for star schema explain plan support) and the level of statistics gathered were different. Oracle has clearly recognized the validity of this database design approach. As a DBA, you too should try to employ Ralph Kimball's dimensional modeling techniques.

STAR SCHEMA CHALLENGES

The more experience you have as an Oracle DBA, the harder you're going find this book's techniques to initially trust. Data warehousing is truly a strange new world for anyone, but especially accomplished DBAs. In particular, star schemas require that you:

- Throw out your OLTP experience baggage.
- Be a good dog willing to learn some new tricks.
- Forget all your Oracle design and tuning Golden Rules.

This is no small challenge. It took me over a year to feel comfortable that what I was doing was right (remember, I had no book such as this to soothe my concerns). All my OLTP DBA counterparts thought I was a "crackpot." But as I explained to them, my database's temporary and rollback tablespaces were each double the size of their entire databases, so I had to use radically different techniques.

Here are some basic star schema data warehouse design guidelines that will sound utterly stupid until you've finished reading this book:

- Do not normalize the database design.
- Do not enable primary or foreign key constraints.
- Create bitmap indexes on every column of every table.
- Use bitmap indexes on columns with lengthy character data.
- Use bitmap indexes on columns with millions of different values.

Unless you can let go of your DBA experience and try these techniques, you're never going to have truly ad-hoc queries that reference billions of rows of data and run in your lifetime. The results will speak for themselves. But, you have to be comfortable that the results are more important than the theories you currently hold to be true. It's not easy.

And to make things even worse, not only do you need to let go of your experience, you must also let go of any SQL and database tuning tools you currently rely on. Most of these tuning tools currently embody two decades of OLTP-based expertise. As such, most of them will give advice or recommendations contrary to the design tenets we'll be following. For kicks, you can use these tools to pseudo-gauge your success—for the more things these tuning tools advise you're doing wrong, the more likely it is that you're doing them right.

A final and equally severe challenge is that you'll have substantially fewer DBAs with whom you can network (i.e., people with whom to discuss your ideas). For example, at EDS, of the dozen or so DBAs for the 7-Eleven account, only two were star schema DBAs. I'd estimate the overall percentage of star schema DBAs to be more like 5%, or 1 in 20 DBAs. So you have notably fewer qualified people with whom you can share and develop ideas. Trust me, it's no fun always being the guy in the know, because then you're not learning anything new from other people you network with.

MODELING STAR SCHEMAS

In dimensional modeling, there are generally only two kinds of tables:

- **Dimensions**—Relatively small, denormalized lookup tables containing business descriptive columns that end-users reference to define their restriction criteria for ad-hoc business intelligence queries.

- **Facts**—Extremely large tables whose primary keys are formed from the concatenation of all the columns that are foreign keys referencing related dimension tables. Facts also possess numerically additive, non-key columns utilized to satisfy calculations required by end-user ad-hoc business intelligence queries.

A simple example of a dimensional data model is shown in Figure 4–1.

Figure 4–1 represents the basic retail store concept for POS information. POS data is gathered directly and automatically at each store's cash registers, which are in fact really just special-purpose computers. At some regular interval, that data is then fed into the corporate information systems—and ultimately the data warehouse.

Figure 4–1 has three dimension tables: PERIOD, LOCATION, and PRODUCT. PERIOD is the time dimension, which almost all star schema designs possess. Keep in mind that most OLTP systems do not have a table for time, but instead have date and timestamp columns where appropriate. But almost all ad-hoc user queries against a star schema will relate or be restricted by some time information. LOCATION is simply the various retail store locations, and PRODUCT represents the items sold by those stores. Remember, the primary mission of dimensions is to provide end-users lots of fields on which to place query restrictions.

Figure 4–1 also has three fact tables: POS_DAY, POS_WEEK, and POS_MONTH. POS_DAY simply represents the sales data for a given store on a given day. POS_WEEK and POS_MONTH are aggregates, or summarizations, of their underlying fact tables. So, POS_WEEK is the daily sales rolled up by week, and POS_MONTH

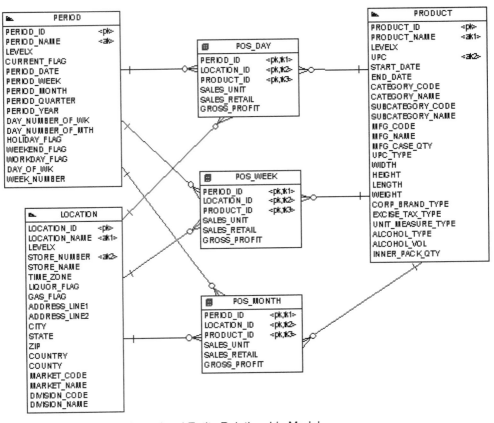

Figure 4–1   Example Dimensional Entity Relationship Model

is sales rolled up by month. Obviously, a user query possessing the right granularity such that it can utilize the POS_MONTH table will run faster than the same query against the POS_DAY table. Not convinced of that? Well, POS_MONTH is about 30 times smaller than POS_DAY. Of course, smaller in data warehousing terms— POS_MONTH is still nearly a billion rows.

Look again at the fact tables. These tables can be huge, with row counts easily on the order of 10^9 to 10^{12}, or larger. That's hundreds of millions to hundreds of billions of rows! Of course, with any object of that size, the DBA is going to most likely use partitioning. Yet notice how we did not try to relate the actual physical implementation in the data model. This is critical as the DBA has an ever-increasing number of implementation options for both facts and their aggregates with the newer versions of Oracle.

One question that very often arises at my data warehousing presentations is: Which data modeling tool is best for data warehousing? The answer is simple: your brain. While all the various data modeling tools have their pros and cons, none of them is so intrinsically better than the rest for data warehousing as to rate a recommendation. For example, none of the current data modeling tools cleanly diagrams or records any meta-data regarding how facts and aggregates might use partitioning and/or materialized views. Don't get me wrong; I'm a huge advocate of data modeling. But for data warehousing, I find that the physical data model is useful merely as a roadmap for the ETL programmers. The real physical object implementation is far too complex for modeling tools to handle.

Another question I often get is: How do I transform my OLTP database design into a dimensional model? The short, cop-out answer is to let the business analysts familiar with the data and business intelligence tool model your star schemas. That leaves you, as the DBA, to concentrate on the more physical implementation issues. That's exactly what I did at 7-Eleven and it worked like a charm. But for those DBAs who must also perform dimensional modeling, here are some basic steps for transforming an OLTP model into a star schema design:

- Denormalize lookup relationships.
- Denormalize parent/child relationships.
- Create and populate a time dimension.
- Create hierarchies of data within dimensions.
- Consider using surrogate or meaningless keys.

AVOID SNOWFLAKES

Look again at the dimensions in Figure 4–1. These three tables are clearly denormalized (i.e., in zero normal form), as they should be. But DBA instincts being what they are, far too often mistakenly attempt to normalize star schema designs. In effect, they try to

apply OLTP logic to their data warehouse. In data warehousing par-
lance, such forced normalization attempts are called snowflakes.
Let's look at a snowflake example to avoid.

First, the PRODUCT dimension clearly violates third normal
form (i.e., a non-key column depends on another non-key column) in
three places:

- MFG_NAME depends entirely on MFG_CODE.
- CATEGORY_NAME depends entirely on CATGEORY_CODE.
- SUBCATEGORY_NAME depends entirely on
  SUBCATEGORY_CODE.

Likewise, the LOCATION dimension also violates third normal
form in two places:

- MARKET_NAME depends entirely on MARKET_CODE.
- DIVISION_NAME depends entirely on DIVISION_NAME.

Finally, the LOCATION dimension also violates first normal
form (i.e., no column is an array or repeats groups of values) in two
places:

- ADDRESS_LINE1
- ADDRESS_LINE2

This clearly represents an array of address lines, which is a
repeating group. So what you end up with is a model that is in zero
normal form. Remember, normal forms are cumulative, meaning you
cannot be in one normal form if you violate its predecessor. Therefore, if you've violated first normal form, you cannot be at any higher
normalization level.

When you apply OLTP skills to star schemas, you end up with a
model like that shown in Figure 4–2.

So what does Figure 4–2 accomplish? The data model has been
normalized, thus the resulting database will save a few bytes of inexpensive disk space. The problem is that the ad-hoc user queries will
now take forever to run. The key problem is that by adding all these
snowflake tables, the Oracle optimizer is confused into thinking this
is in fact an OLTP database and not a star schema. This is a waste of
disk space. Had space been saved in a fact table, then it's probably a

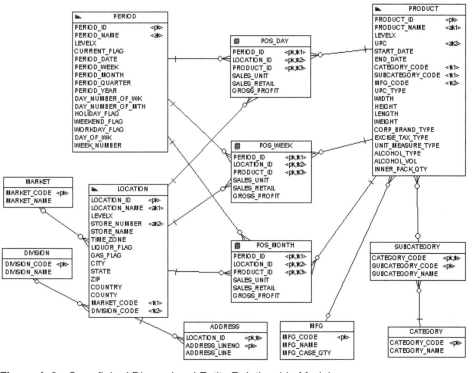

Figure 4–2   Snowflaked Dimensional Entity Relationship Model

worthwhile endeavor. But the dimension tables are relatively small, so saving space here at the expense of the extra joins and confusing the Oracle optimizer is not advisable.

Of course, someone will inevitably ask, "Why can't I build the database like Figure 4–2 and then just simply create view definitions to reassemble the snowflaked dimensions?" The short answer is because it doesn't work. A view definition is really nothing more than a pre-canned query. So, that pre-canned query is extrapolated and merged into your query at runtime. Thus, the view only hides the design from the user—not the optimizer. So, you end up with queries that the optimizer cannot handle utilizing Oracle's latest and greatest star schema features. In other words, the query takes forever to run.

To recap, snowflakes are bad because they:

- Add additional levels of JOIN complexity (i.e., add more tables to JOIN).

- Complicate end-user query construction as there are now more tables to choose from, unless view definitions are used to combine multiple tables into singular, flat objects from which to select.
- Are mishandled as OLTP data by the Oracle query optimizer (i.e., bad explain plan).
- Save a little cheap disk space at the cost of much longer query runtimes.

DIMENSIONAL HIERARCHIES

One of the hardest star schema design concepts to initially grasp is that of dimensional hierarchies. I've found more confusion in this one area alone than with all other star schema design issues combined. However, dimensional hierarchies are truly one of the easiest star schema design concepts to understand—once explained properly.

First, note I said the "concept" of dimensional hierarchies. Oracle 8i and 9i both support the CREATE DIMENSION statement for actually documenting the existence of a dimensional hierarchy. Note that this statement merely creates meta-data within the Oracle data dictionary to describe the dimensional hierarchy such that materialized view query rewrites work properly. There is no physical database object created by the CREATE DIMENSION statement. But we'll discuss this in a later chapter where we specifically address using materialized views. For now, we mean implementing a dimensional hierarchy manually using plain, old tables (i.e., without using Oracle's CREATE DIMENSION statement).

Look back at the dimension tables in Figure 4–1. Each has a third column of LEVELX. This is the dimensional hierarchy column. What does this column mean or do?

According to Oracle: "A dimension defines a parent–child relationship between pairs of column sets, where all the columns of a column set must come from the same table." That's the hard way (it seems) of saying that each dimension table represents multiple types of information (i.e., different record types) as represented by the columns that contain data for a given row.

Let's look at a specific example. The LEVELX column of the PERIOD dimension from Figure 4–1 has the following distinct values:

- DAY
- WEEK
- MONTH
- QUARTER
- YEAR

Let's assume that our end-user is using a business intelligence tool and wants to use the PERIOD dimension to specify a query based on a quarter. Only certain columns from the PERIOD table apply—in fact, just the PERIOD_QUARTER column. All other columns should not have values. If the query focus was month, then only the columns PERIOD_QUARTER and PERIOD_MONTH should have values. In effect, we're saying that a column's mandatory versus optional property depends on the value of another column from the same row of data. This requires all non-primary and non-unique key columns for the dimension table to be optional. This in turn requires the DBA to write some pretty complex table check constraints.

For instance, for the PERIOD table from Figure 4–1, the table-level check constraint necessary is:

```
CONSTRAINT PERIOD_LEVELX
  CHECK ( ( LEVELX = 'YEAR' )
         OR
         ( LEVELX = 'QUARTER' AND
           PERIOD_QUARTER IS NOT NULL )
         OR
         ( LEVELX = 'MONTH' AND
           PERIOD_QUARTER IS NOT NULL AND
           PERIOD_MONTH IS NOT NULL )
         OR
         ( LEVELX = 'WEEK' AND
           PERIOD_QUARTER IS NOT NULL AND
           PERIOD_MONTH IS NOT NULL AND
           PERIOD_WEEK IS NOT NULL AND
           WEEK_NUMBER IS NOT NULL )
         OR
         ( LEVELX = 'DAY'  AND
           PERIOD_WEEK IS NOT NULL AND
           PERIOD_MONTH IS NOT NULL AND
           PERIOD_QUARTER IS NOT NULL AND
           DAY_NUMBER_OF_WK IS NOT NULL AND
           DAY_NUMBER_OF_MTH IS NOT NULL AND
```

```
                    HOLIDAY_FLAG IS NOT NULL AND
                    WEEKEND_FLAG IS NOT NULL AND
                    WORKDAY_FLAG IS NOT NULL AND
                    DAY_OF_WK IS NOT NULL AND
                    WEEK_NUMBER IS NOT NULL )
              )
```

I have two final thoughts regarding dimensional hierarchies. First, most data modeling tools generally will not help you with writing complex table check constraints such as this example. Second, the check constraint should enforce whatever business rules the business intelligence software requires. Don't get caught up in an opinion on this one. Just build whatever is necessary.

QUERYING STAR SCHEMAS

End-users will generally utilize business intelligence tools to submit report requests. In Oracle terms, each request may generate a series of SELECT statements necessary to construct the complete report. For example, your users' business intelligence tool may have a server process of its own that processes the returned SQL SELECT results using advanced OLAP functions and logic not yet found within Oracle. So as the DBA, you'll only be able to see the intermediate queries by scanning the SGA. Not to worry, though, for generally if we can make the intermediate queries faster, the overall report execution will improve as well.

A typical user query might be something like the following: How much beer and coffee did we sell in our Dallas stores during December 1998? Using our example dimensional model in Figure 4–1, a typical ad-hoc business intelligence intermediate query submitted to Oracle might look something like:

```
SELECT prod.category_name,
       sum (fact.sales_unit) Units,
       sum (fact.sales_retail) Retail
FROM   pos_day              fact,
       period               per,
       location             loc,
       product              prod
WHERE  fact.period_id       = per.period_id
  AND  fact.location_id     = loc.location_id
  AND  fact.product_id      = prod.product_id
```

```
AND   per.levelx         = 'DAY'
AND   per.period_month   = 12
AND   per.period_year    = 1998
AND   loc.levelx         = 'STORE'
AND   loc.city           = 'DALLAS'
AND   loc.state          = 'TX'
AND   prod.levelx        = 'ITEM'
AND   prod.category_name in ('BEER','COFFEE')
GROUP BY prod.category_name;
```

with results of:

```
CATEGORY_NAME                  UNITS         RETAIL
----------------------  ------------  --------------
BEER                          11,613       64,490.81
COFFEE                        22,808       20,462.92
```

Even this example yields key insights into what the DBA can expect in the way of queries against star schema warehouses. In general, a star schema SELECT will:

- Use GROUP functions and therefore GROUP BY.
- Contain a JOIN of a fact with one or more dimensions.
- Possess lots of WHERE restrictions using dimension columns.
- Scan lots of rows to return relatively few rows of results.

Conversely, business intelligence tool-generated SQL may target the wrong level of table summarization (i.e., example query should have used the month table instead of the day table, and therefore offers opportunities for tuning or utilizing query rewrites).

That's it. Star schema queries are just that simple. In fact, they are nothing more than table searches via some lookup tables. Oracle has been able to handle queries of this nature for years, but the sheer size of data warehouses make this something altogether different.

FACT TABLE OPTIONS

Fact tables are huge. They are so huge that it should come as no surprise that much of your success will depend on how you implement your facts. Thus, I'm offering as general DBA advice my best Joe

Friday from *Dragnet* imitation: "Just the facts …," meaning if you get just the facts done right, you're well on the road to success.

But to do this right, you must look beyond just size. At any given time, fact tables will fall into one of three states:

- Being queried (covered in Chapter 5)
- Being loaded (covered in Chapters 6 and 7)
- Being managed (covered in Chapter 8)

The key point is that to be successful, fact table implementations must accommodate the different requirements of all three states. Far too often, DBAs concentrate on just one or two of these states, and end up with a sub-optimal solution. Or worse yet, they apply misguided "common sense" rather than empirical evidence in making their selections.

Let's start by identifying our basic options for implementing fact tables:

- Non-partitioned, heap-organized
- Range-partitioned, heap-organized
- List-partitioned, heap-organized
- Hash-partitioned, heap-organized
- Composite range, hash-partitioned, heap-organized
- Composite range, list-partitioned, heap-organized
- Non-partitioned, index-organized
- Range-partitioned, index-organized

For each of these implementation choices, you have the following additional choices for whether the table's indexes are:

- Non-partitioned
- Partitioned locally
- Partitioned globally

Finally, both the tables and indexes can be either:

- Logging versus no logging
- Parallel versus non-parallel
- Compressed versus non-compressed

That makes for one heck of a lot of choices. Do you really know which is best by merely picking from these lists? I sure don't. But if we reexamine these choices with the proper importance weightings from our three states, the process becomes much easier.

So which of the three states would you label most important? This is actually the most critical distinction in making the proper implementation selection. More often than not, the naturally proposed answer is the query state. But for the moment (or at least until you read Chapter 5), trust me when I say that I can get ultra-fast queries with near identical runtimes utilizing any of these options, as long as I get the right explain plan. So now which state becomes most important?

The second most often proposed answer is the loading state. The idea is that unless you partition, you cannot drop indexes, load data, and recreate indexes in a timely fashion. But this is a data management response to what is being termed a loading question. What I mean is that dropping and recreating indexes quickly has more to do with determining partition size, which is really a data management issue. For example, I could choose to partition my tables and indexes, but only create two partitions per object. This would only cut the index creation time in half, so it's really not a great choice. Therefore, this has nothing to do with the data loading architecture.

If you have not guessed by now, it's the management state that should drive your fact table implementation selection. First, most companies do not have an infinite budget for their data warehouses, so at some point, data must be archived. For example, at 7-Eleven, we kept 60 months of data online, with the plan to archive by month once we had reached our limit.

Now, if you choose the simple, non-partitioned, heap-organized table, how would you archive data? The answer is: with a very slow and painful delete command. Moreover, you'd screw up your non-partitioned b-tree index structures, requiring a potential rebuild. So for archival purposes, you should partition by some time dimension criteria such as week or month. That of course would also aid your loading process index drop and build since you'd operate only those few, smaller partitions that were current.

Okay, so partitioned it is (covered in Chapter 8), but which one? The answer is simple. First, let's agree that index-organized tables (IOTs) are great for OLTP lookup scenarios, but make a poor choice for huge fact tables. Trust me; don't go this way unless you like lots of elevator music—because you'll be calling Oracle support more than is necessary. Second, let's agree that lots of small date range buckets could be implemented with equal ease using either range or list partitioning. That cuts our choices in half to just:

• Range-partitioned, heap-organized
• List-partitioned, heap-organized
• Composite range, hash-partitioned, heap-organized
• Composite range, list-partitioned, heap-organized

Now, remember back in Chapter 3, "Hardware Architecture," when we discussed hardware, specifically the number of CPUs and degree of parallel operations permitted? Well, a lot of DBAs assume that they must sub-partition to get the highest degree of parallel queries possible. But, there are two flaws with this premise. First, does your data lend itself to sub-partitioning? For example, I tried hashed sub-partitions with 7-Eleven's data warehouse. I partitioned by range on my period identifier, making each partition contain a week's worth of data. Then I hash sub-partitioned on my product identifier. The idea was that similar products would hash into the same sub-partitions, thus queries on classes of products (such as beer) would only reference those sub-partitions. Sounds good, right? But I had overlooked the nature of my data. The product identifiers were evenly distributed across the entire product identifier domain. Thus, hashing merely spread my data equally across all the sub-partitions and required an extra level of sub-partition operations to obtain the exact same data. So, my queries took twice as long. Needless to say, I went back to just partitions without sub-partitions.

Second, does your hardware have sufficient CPU bandwidth to handle the extra parallel operations permitted by sub-partitioning? If you have 32 processors, but also have 100 people concurrently running reports, then using the parallel feature at the table level is probably already overkill. But I see this same mistake at over half the data warehouses I visit. The DBA assumes that more than one CPU mandates turning on parallel queries. But unless you have more CPUs than your concurrent report load, the parallel feature is a loaded gun waiting to go off in your face. Use it judiciously. Thus, sub-partitioning for an added level of parallel operations is not the "slam dunk" people automatically think it is.

So, our partitioning options (again, covered in detail in Chapter 8) are really quite simple:

- Range-partitioned, heap-organized
- List-partitioned, heap-organized

As always, the best choice will depend on your specific requirements, skill set, comfort level, and the nature of your data.

WHEN STARS IMPLODE

I've learned one important and somewhat humbling lesson during my four years of presenting my data warehousing papers at shows and conferences: Even DBAs are not infallible! I've always assumed that if a feature existed in Oracle, the typical DBA would use it correctly. But, I've run into hundreds of people who claim that their data warehouse must be special because they cannot get star schema techniques to work for them. Even more disturbing, they just assume they've hit the "brick wall" since their data warehouses are so big. The problem is that 99% of the time, they're not yet even a terabyte in size when they throw in the towel. So how and why does this happen?

The only explanation I can find is that most of these DBAs often take issue with one or two concepts presented in this book and choose not to implement them. They wrongly assume that doing 95% of these techniques will yield almost the same great results. It definitely will not. If you skip even what you consider to be the most trivial step, you will never reap the big rewards. I've seen and heard of these same techniques working on star schema data warehouses approaching 100 terabytes in size. So they can and do work. But you must have faith and implement the whole package.

I've found that it helps on those occasions when a DBA has issues with some of my advice to show him or her other references offering similar or the same advice. So here are a few Oracle white papers I strongly recommend (with the most important ones in bold):

- **"Star Queries in Oracle 8"**, June 1997
- "Data Warehouse Performance Enhancements with Oracle 9i", April 2001
- "Oracle 9i Performance and Scalability in DSS Environments", April 2001
- **"Key Data Warehousing Features in Oracle 9i: A comparative Performance Analysis"**, September 2001
- **"Query Optimization in Oracle 9i"**, February 2002

You can download all these papers from either Oracle's Metalink Support (*www.oracle.com/support/metalink*) or Oracle's Technology Network (*technet.oracle.com*).

CHAPTER 5

Tuning Ad-Hoc Queries

This is the single most important chapter in the entire book. Here I'll explain how to get lightning-fast queries, even though you have no idea what those queries may look like (i.e., truly ad-hoc reports). This is also going to be the hardest chapter for many DBAs to accept because the advice flies so contrary to popular belief. But rest assured, this is the only way to go.

A really good question to ask at this point is: Why am I covering ad-hoc query tuning before other major topics such as loading data? The answer is simple: If end-users cannot quickly view reports on the data, then the data warehouse is a bust. In fact, you can judge your data warehouse's success by simply asking the following: Do the end-users run many more ad-hoc reports than they had originally planned? If the answer is yes, then you've hit a home run. When ad-hoc reports run quickly, the users can perform much more detailed "what-if" analyses and drill much deeper into the massive amounts of data to find better business answers. So, more is better.

Another way to look at this is to think in terms of this nursery rhyme-type question: How much data would a data miner mine if a data miner could mine data? Again, the answer is really quite simple: as much as time permits. So, if ad-hoc reports run quickly, they'll naturally dig deeper. But note that we are talking about data warehouses with massive amounts of data, so "quickly" is really a very relative term. If you remember, in Chapter 1, we examined the criteria of what constitutes a data warehouse. The end-users are usually executives or very senior managers making monumental business decisions. As such, a report that answers a truly strategic question and runs in less than 30 minutes is most likely acceptable. Of course, if you follow these techniques, your ad-hoc reports will run in much less time than that.

Finally, in Chapter 4 we examined the concept of fact versus dimension tables and how to model them with data. I'd like to augment those definitions to include some query-specific terminology:

- **Dimension tables**—Generally queried in business terms with high selectivity to find relatively few lookup value matches that are then used to query against the fact table.
- **Fact tables**—Must be selectively queried since they often have hundreds of millions to billions of rows; even full table scans utilizing parallel query are too big for most systems.

KEY TUNING REQUIREMENTS

In a nutshell, these are the requirements for lightning-fast ad-hoc star schema queries:

- Oracle 8i or 9i
- Star transformation explain plan on queries
- Correct INIT.ORA settings
- Bitmap indexes (and lots of them)
- Cost-based optimizer (i.e., statistics)

Of all these, the star transformation explain plan is our ultimate goal. In fact, everything else is merely a prerequisite for the star transformation explain plan. In other words, you cannot get the star transformation explain plan without the proper INIT.ORA settings, bitmap indexes, and cost-based optimization.

As I've said several times now, you must fully meet all these requirements to succeed. Failure to implement any portion of the recommended advice will definitely not achieve the desired results; in fact, it may be worse than any other configuration. So, you have to adopt a "take it or leave it" approach.

If you re-examine Chapter 2's section on Oracle version options, I made a very clear case why you must be on Oracle 8i or 9i to succeed. To recap, only these latest versions of Oracle offer:

- Reliable and efficient partitioning
- Reliable and efficient bitmap indexes
- Star transformation explain plan support
- Reliable and efficient statistics for cost-based optimization
- Reliable and efficient histograms for cost-based optimization
- Reliable, efficient, and easy-to-use parallel query and DML

While Oracle 8.0 offers many or most of these key features, each was either too new or as yet unperfected. You may succeed with Oracle 8.0, but the recommendation is 8i or 9i all the way. Again, it does not matter if your source OLTP systems are in different versions of Oracle than your data warehouse. With data warehouses, you'll generally be far better off riding the bleeding edge of Oracle technology.

STAR OPTIMIZATION EVOLUTION

There are several ways to optimize a query against a star schema design. But, the results are radically different in terms of runtime performance. Let's examine the evolution of these star schema query optimization techniques, their basic explain plan formats, and their performance results. We'll use the same example query from Chapter 4: How much beer and coffee did we sell in our Dallas stores during December 1998? The SQL code is as follows:

```
SELECT  prod.category_name,
        sum (fact.sales_unit) Units,
        sum (fact.sales_retail) Retail
FROM    pos_day              fact,
        period               per,
        location             loc,
        product              prod
WHERE   fact.period_id     = per.period_id
  AND   fact.location_id   = loc.location_id
  AND   fact.product_id    = prod.product_id
  AND   per.levelx         = 'DAY'
```

```
AND   per.period_month   = 12
AND   per.period_year    = 1998
AND   loc.levelx         = 'STORE'
AND   loc.city           = 'DALLAS'
AND   loc.state          = 'TX'
AND   prod.levelx        = 'ITEM'
AND   prod.category_name in ('BEER','COFFEE')
GROUP BY prod.category_name;
```

First-Generation

First-generation star schema query optimization consists of first joining a fact table to a dimension table and then iteratively joining the
intermediate results table to each remaining dimension table. That
translates into nested loops, and most DBAs already know that nested
loops generally mean slow performance. Oracle 6 offered only first-
generation star schema query optimization.

An explain plan for first-generation star schema optimization
would look like Figure 5–1.

Operation	Object Name	Rows	Bytes	Cost	Object Node	In/Out	PStart	PStop
SELECT STATEMENT Optimizer Mode=HINT: RULE								
SORT GROUP BY								
NESTED LOOPS								
NESTED LOOPS								
NESTED LOOPS								
TABLE ACCESS FULL	PERIOD							
TABLE ACCESS BY INDEX ROWID	POS_DAY							
INDEX RANGE SCAN	POS_DAY_PK							
TABLE ACCESS BY INDEX ROWID	PRODUCT							
INDEX UNIQUE SCAN	PRODUCT_PK							
TABLE ACCESS BY INDEX ROWID	LOCATION							
INDEX UNIQUE SCAN	LOCATION_PK							

Figure 5–1   Explain Plan for First-Generation Star Query Optimization

Example runtime statistics for a fact table with 7 million rows
were found to be:

- 6,550 physical reads
- 698,742 logical reads
- 273 CPUs used by session
- 17.125 seconds elapsed time

There is absolutely no value in using this method for data warehousing. I merely disclose this information so that you understand the complete history of star schema tuning.

Second-Generation

Second-generation star schema query optimization consists of first Cartesian joining all dimension tables into one intermediate results table, and then joining that table to the fact table. This was Oracle 7's STAR hint. Just the fact that it does repetitive Cartesian joins should be enough to eliminate this choice for most people. Remember that Cartesian joining means combining every row of one table with every row from another table. That means a Cartesian join is a multi-table `SELECT` without a `WHERE` clause condition connecting those tables. Cartesian joining always means slow performance and should be avoided.

An explain plan for second-generation star schema optimization would look like Figure 5–2.

Operation	Object Name	Rows	Bytes	Cost	Object Node	In/Out	PStart	PStop
⊟ SELECT STATEMENT Optimizer Mode=CHOOSE		1		48				
⊟ SORT GROUP BY		1	169	48				
⊟ NESTED LOOPS		1	169	35				
⊟ MERGE JOIN CARTESIAN		1	143	32				
⊟ MERGE JOIN CARTESIAN		1	92	20.7987814097776				
⊟ TABLE ACCESS BY INDEX ROWID	LOCATION	1	46	2.43108316469135				
⊟ BITMAP CONVERSION TO ROWIDS								
⊟ BITMAP AND								
BITMAP INDEX SINGLE VALUE	LOCATION_B03							
BITMAP INDEX SINGLE VALUE	LOCATION_B11							
⊟ BUFFER SORT		17	782	18.3676982450863				
⊟ TABLE ACCESS BY INDEX ROWID	PRODUCT	17	782	20.7987814097776				
⊟ BITMAP CONVERSION TO ROWIDS								
⊟ BITMAP AND								
BITMAP INDEX SINGLE VALUE	PRODUCT_B03							
⊟ BITMAP OR								
BITMAP INDEX SINGLE VALUE	PRODUCT_B08							
BITMAP INDEX SINGLE VALUE	PRODUCT_B08							
⊟ BUFFER SORT		1	51	11.2012185902224				
TABLE ACCESS FULL	PERIOD	1	51	11				
⊟ TABLE ACCESS BY INDEX ROWID	POS_DAY	1	26	3				
INDEX UNIQUE SCAN	POS_DAY_PK	1		2				

Figure 5–2   Explain Plan for Second-Generation Star Query Optimization

Example runtime statistics for a fact table with 7 million rows were found to be:

- 2,923 physical reads
- 156,154,547 logical reads

- 29,414 CPUs used by session
- 296.782 seconds elapsed time

Yes, that's over 156 million logical reads, with over 107 times as much CPU time and over 17 times as long to run! There is absolutely no case under which I can recommend using the STAR hint. It stinks. Don't use it.

Third-Generation

Third-generation star schema query optimization consists of Oracle's new, patented star transformation optimization technique, introduced in Oracle 8.0 and perfected by Oracle 9i. This method of accessing a fact table leverages the strengths of Oracle's bitmap indexes, bitmap operations, and hash joins. However, *you must closely follow the advice of all subsequent sections regarding both initialization parameters and indexes to obtain such explain plans*. In short and at a minimum, you must create a bitmap index on each fact table's dimension table's foreign key columns. In our example, that would mean:

- CREATE BITMAP INDEX POS_DAY_B1 ON POS_DAY (PERIOD_ID)
- CREATE BITMAP INDEX POS_DAY_B2 ON POS_DAY (LOCATION_ID)
- CREATE BITMAP INDEX POS_DAY_B3 ON POS_DAY (PRODUCT_ID)

The entire index design will be discussed in more detail later. When done correctly, the explain plan for third-generation star schema optimization should look like Figure 5–3.

Example runtime statistics for a fact table with 7 million rows were found to be:

- 3,410 physical reads
- 22,655 logical reads
- 33 CPUs used by session
- 0.641 seconds elapsed time

Operation	Object Name	Rows	Bytes	Cost	Object Node	In/Out	PStart	PStop
SELECT STATEMENT Optimizer Mode=CHOOSE		1		41				
┌ RECURSIVE EXECUTION	SYS_LE_2_0							
┌ TEMP TABLE TRANSFORMATION								
┌ SORT GROUP BY		1	60	41				
┌ HASH JOIN		1	60	29				
┌ TABLE ACCESS BY INDEX ROWID	POS_DAY	11.6591057704	303.13675003	23.810845166				
┌ BITMAP CONVERSION TO ROWIDS								
┌ BITMAP AND								
┌ BITMAP MERGE								
┌ BITMAP KEY ITERATION								
┌ TABLE ACCESS BY INDEX ROWID	PERIOD	1	51	2.3187859461				
┌ BITMAP CONVERSION TO ROWIDS								
┌ BITMAP AND								
┌ BITMAP INDEX SINGLE VALUE	PERIOD_B03							
└ BITMAP INDEX SINGLE VALUE	PERIOD_B07							
BITMAP INDEX RANGE SCAN	POS_DAY_B1							
┌ BITMAP MERGE								
┌ BITMAP KEY ITERATION								
┌ TABLE ACCESS BY INDEX ROWID	LOCATION	1	46	2.4310831646				
┌ BITMAP CONVERSION TO ROWIDS								
┌ BITMAP AND								
┌ BITMAP INDEX SINGLE VALUE	LOCATION_B03							
└ BITMAP INDEX SINGLE VALUE	LOCATION_B11							
BITMAP INDEX RANGE SCAN	POS_DAY_B2							
┌ BITMAP MERGE								
┌ BITMAP KEY ITERATION								
┌ TABLE ACCESS FULL	SYS_TEMP_0FD9D6604_356F6A	1	13	2				
└ BITMAP INDEX RANGE SCAN	POS_DAY_B3							
└ TABLE ACCESS FULL	SYS_TEMP_0FD9D6604_356F6A	17	578	2				

Figure 5–3   Explain Plan for Third-Generation Star Query Optimization

How does it achieve such stellar results (no pun intended)? Oracle essentially rewrites the query as a non-correlated sub-query (shown below) and performs the explain plan in two distinct steps. First, it uses bitmap indexes on both the dimension and fact tables to greatly reduce the number of fact rows to return. Second, it joins the resulting limited set of fact rows to the dimension tables. This is a highly efficient and desirable explain plan to execute.

```
SELECT …
FROM    pos_day              fact
WHERE   fact.period_id     in (
        SELECT period_id
        FROM    period
        WHERE   levelx       = 'DAY'
        AND     period_month = 12
        AND     period_year  = 1998 )
  AND   fact.location_id   in (
        SELECT location_id
        FROM    location
        WHERE   levelx = 'STORE'
        AND     city   = 'DALLAS'
        AND     state  = 'TX' )
  AND   fact.product_id    in (
        SELECT product_id
```

```
FROM    product
WHERE   levelx         = 'ITEM'
AND     category_name in ('BEER','COFFEE') )
...;
```

Look again at Figure 5–3. While this particular plan shows a temporary table being used in the star transformation process, this is not always the case. The general format of a star transformation is:

- Hash join
  - Table access by index ROWID for fact
    - Bitmap AND
      - Bitmap MERGE
        - Table access by index ROWID for Dimension #1
          - Bitmap "AND"
            - Bitmap index scan
            - Bitmap index scan
            - … Repeats …
      - Bitmap index range scan for fact
    - Bitmap MERGE
      - Table access by index ROWID for Dimension #2
        - Bitmap "AND"
          - Bitmap index scan
          - Bitmap index scan
          - … Repeats …
      - Bitmap index range scan for fact
- … Repeats …

As you'll see in the following section on index design, this optimization technique relies extensively on bitmap indexes for both dimension and fact tables. Look again at the explain plan: Only simple bitmap index scans appear—no b-tree index scans. If you get a plan with b-trees, you have not obtained a star transformation and the runtime will be substantially longer. Bitmap indexes are our best friends in data warehousing.

Fourth-Generation

Fourth-generation star schema query optimization consists of Oracle's new bitmap join indexes, introduced in Oracle 9i. Bitmap join indexes create a bitmap index on one table based on the columns of another table or tables. The idea is that bitmap join indexes hold pre-computed join results in a very efficient index structure. In theory, this should be the best possible route to go. The problem is that when people attempt to use this type of index, it can yield varying results, some of which are quite undesirable.

The first and most natural attempt at using bitmap join indexes is to replace existing third-generation solution bitmap indexes on the fact table's dimension table's foreign key columns. For example, instead of creating a bitmap index on each of our fact table's dimension table's foreign key columns, we would instead create bitmap join indexes. In DDL terms for our example, we would replace:

```
CREATE BITMAP INDEX POS_DAY_B1 ON POS_DAY (PERIOD_ID)
```

with:

```
CREATE BITMAP INDEX POS_DAY_BJ1 ON POS_DAY (PER.PERIOD_ID)
FROM POS_DAY POS, PERIOD PER
WHERE POS.PERIOD_ID = PER.PERIOD_ID
```

An explain plan for fourth-generation star schema optimization would look like Figure 5–4.

Example runtime statistics for a fact table with 7 million rows were found to be:

- 56,624 physical reads
- 60,714 logical reads
- 470 CPUs used by session
- 12.14 seconds elapsed time

Wait just a minute. What happened? This was supposed to make things better, not worse. Look again at Figure 5–4. Although Oracle 9i's optimizer utilized the new bitmap join indexes, it also reverted back to using nested loops and b-tree indexes. And for most data warehouses, we never want to see b-tree indexes in our query explain

Operation	Object Name	Rows	Bytes	Cost	Object Node	In/Out	PStart	PStop
⊟ SELECT STATEMENT Optimizer Mode=CHOOSE		1		40				
⊟ SORT GROUP BY		1	169	40				
⊟ NESTED LOOPS		1	169	27				
⊟ HASH JOIN		1	123	25				
⊟ TABLE ACCESS BY INDEX ROWID	LOCATION	1	46	2.43108316469135				
⊟ BITMAP CONVERSION TO ROWIDS								
⊟ BITMAP AND								
BITMAP INDEX SINGLE VALUE	LOCATION_B03							
BITMAP INDEX SINGLE VALUE	LOCATION_B11							
⊟ HASH JOIN		89	6 K	22				
⊟ TABLE ACCESS BY INDEX ROWID	PERIOD	1	51	2.31878594617595				
⊟ BITMAP CONVERSION TO ROWIDS								
⊟ BITMAP AND								
BITMAP INDEX SINGLE VALUE	PERIOD_B03							
BITMAP INDEX SINGLE VALUE	PERIOD_B07							
⊟ TABLE ACCESS BY INDEX ROWID	POS_DAY_BJ1	720.7146	18 K	17.9502403409479				
⊟ BITMAP CONVERSION TO ROWIDS								
⊟ BITMAP AND								
⊟ BITMAP MERGE								
BITMAP INDEX RANGE SCAN	POS_DAY_BJ1_BJ1							
⊟ BITMAP MERGE								
BITMAP INDEX RANGE SCAN	POS_DAY_BJ1_BJ3							
⊟ TABLE ACCESS BY INDEX ROWID	PRODUCT	1	46	2				
INDEX UNIQUE SCAN	PRODUCT_PK	10 K		1				

Figure 5–4   Flawed Explain Plan for Fourth-Generation Star Query Optimization

plans—they'll run orders of magnitude slower than if using exclusively bitmaps. And for Oracle 8i, the explain plan would not have used any of the new bitmap join indexes. It would instead do a full table scan of our fact table! Lesson learned: A successful fourth-generation solution must be built *on* a third-generation foundation, not instead of. In other words, we need both bitmap indexes from above. We should let the Oracle query optimizer decide what's best. When done correctly, the explain plan should look like Figure 5–5.

Operation	Object Name	Rows	Bytes	Cost	Object Node	In/Out	PStart	PStop
⊟ SELECT STATEMENT Optimizer Mode=CHOOSE		13		50				
⊟ SORT GROUP BY		13	936	50				
⊟ HASH JOIN		13	936	38				
⊟ TABLE ACCESS BY INDEX ROWID	PRODUCT	17	782	12.8445899286171				
⊟ BITMAP CONVERSION TO ROWIDS								
⊟ BITMAP AND								
⊟ BITMAP OR								
BITMAP INDEX SINGLE VALUE	PRODUCT_B08							
BITMAP INDEX SINGLE VALUE	PRODUCT_B08							
BITMAP INDEX SINGLE VALUE	PRODUCT_B03							
⊟ TABLE ACCESS BY INDEX ROWID	POS_DAY_BJ2	1 K	38 K	22.0878020973911				
⊟ BITMAP CONVERSION TO ROWIDS								
⊟ BITMAP AND								
⊟ BITMAP MERGE								
⊟ BITMAP KEY ITERATION								
⊟ TABLE ACCESS BY INDEX ROWID	PERIOD	1	51	2.31878594617595				
⊟ BITMAP CONVERSION TO ROWIDS								
⊟ BITMAP AND								
BITMAP INDEX SINGLE VALUE	PERIOD_B03							
BITMAP INDEX SINGLE VALUE	PERIOD_B07							
BITMAP INDEX RANGE SCAN	POS_DAY_BJ2_B1							
⊟ BITMAP MERGE								
⊟ BITMAP KEY ITERATION								
⊟ TABLE ACCESS BY INDEX ROWID	LOCATION	1	46	2.43108316469135				
⊟ BITMAP CONVERSION TO ROWIDS								
⊟ BITMAP AND								
BITMAP INDEX SINGLE VALUE	LOCATION_B03							
BITMAP INDEX SINGLE VALUE	LOCATION_B11							
BITMAP INDEX RANGE SCAN	POS_DAY_BJ2_B2							
⊟ BITMAP MERGE								
BITMAP INDEX RANGE SCAN	POS_DAY_BJ2_BJ3							

Figure 5–5   Optimal Explain Plan for Fourth-Generation Star Query Optimization

Example runtime statistics for a fact table with 7 million rows were found to be:

- 5,833 physical reads
- 7,111 logical reads
- 79 CPUs used by session
- 3.640 seconds elapsed time

Look again at Figure 5–5. We essentially have the star transformation plan from Figure 5–3 with some very subtle changes. First, the temporary table transformation step is removed near the top of the plan (it's only necessary when temporary tables are being used during the star transformation process). And second, the table access full of the temporary table is replaced near the bottom of the plan with a bitmap range scan of the bitmap join index. But note that it follows our general star transformation pattern and yields a bitmap result to include in the bitmap merge process. So, we have a legitimate star transformation here with simply the addition of a bitmap join index.

Evolutionary Summary

Summarizing our results in Table 5–1, we see that the best overall results are achieved by the third-generation solution: the star transformation. It yields the best mix of physical versus logical I/O, with the lowest CPU usage and elapsed runtime. In other words, the star transformation is our target.

Table 5–1   Comparing Four Generations of Star Query Optimization

Generation	Methodology	Physical Reads	Logical Reads	CPUs Used	Seconds
1	Nested Loops	6,550	698,742	273	17.125
2	Star Join	2,923	156,154,547	29,414	296.782
3	Star Transformation	3,410	22,655	33	0.641
4	Bitmap Join Index	5,833	7,111	79	3.640

STAR TRANSFORMATION QUESTIONS

Now that we've seen the various star schema explain plans and their performance results, let's examine star transformation in a little more detail. Over the past few years, when presenting and speaking on data warehouses, I've been asked quite a few questions regarding star transformation queries. Often I find it's really just a matter of getting comfortable with these radically different concepts for handling large fact tables. Here are some of the most frequently asked questions:

Q: Does the Oracle version matter?

Yes. As I've said numerous times up to this point, you must use Oracle 8i or 9i for best results, although Oracle 8.0 introduced many of the necessary features and may well work for small to mid-sized data warehouses. But, ORA-00600 errors start showing up for both bitmap indexes and partitions as the row counts exceed half a billion.

Q: Does the fact table size matter?

No. The star transformation will work the same if you have a million or a billion rows. The explain plan will be identical and the performance will beat all other alternatives. I've gotten the exact same results using 1/1000 of my UNIX production data on my notebook running Windows.

Q: Will star transformation work when dimension tables are huge?

Yes, kind of. I've had people say they have dimensions with hundreds of millions of rows and they wonder whether star transformation will still work for them. It might, but I really think they have underlying business analysis and dimensional modeling problems. For example, CUSTOMER is often mistakenly viewed as a dimension table for a fact such as CONTRACTS. But really, DEMOGRAPHIC should be the dimension for CONTRACTS.

Q: Will star transformation work for pre-canned reports as well?

Yes. Often, business intelligence users will save and re-run their various reports. Moreover, the data warehouse may also have pre-canned reports written by the IS staff, which may embody those reports everyone needs on a regular basis. It does not matter. The star transformation plan will apply and work for both types of reports.

Q: Will star transformation explain plans always be as easily recognizable as in Figure 5–3 (i.e., contain the phrase transformation)?

No. You should not count on seeing the phase transformation within the explain plan. What's most important is the basic structure of the explain plan, which should look something like this (simplified a bit for readability and to be generically more accurate across the various Oracle versions):

- Hash join
- Table access by index ROWID for fact
  - Bitmap AND
    - Bitmap MERGE
      - Table access by index ROWID for Dimension #1
        - Bitmap "AND"
          - Bitmap index scan
          - Bitmap index scan
          - … Repeats …
      - Bitmap index range scan for fact
    - Bitmap MERGE
      - Table access by index ROWID for Dimension #2
        - Bitmap "AND"
          - Bitmap index scan
          - Bitmap index scan
          - … Repeats …
      - Bitmap index range scan for fact
    - … Repeats …

Q: Isn't parallel query with full table scans better?

No. Why would you want to scan a billion rows in parallel when all you need is a few hundred thousand on which to run a calculation? This is a prime example of people reading an Oracle quote like "It's better to do a full table scan in parallel than to traverse an index b-tree" and applying it with reckless abandon. Use common sense. Use the star transformation. Learn to apply blanket Oracle quotes with caution.

Q: But isn't parallel query with star transformation better?

Yes, sometimes. If you have a fact table that is a billion rows and neither partitioned nor parallel, star transformation will still run lightning-fast. Partitioning may shave off a few seconds or minutes. And, parallel query may shave off even a few more seconds or minutes. But note that neither will provide an order of magnitude improvement. The star transformation plan will be the same, with just some minor differences in the columns for object node, operation in/out, partition start, and partition stop. That's it. The moral of the story is that if you can get it right for the non-parallel and non-partitioned world, you can improve on it with these features as well. But they are merely icing on the cake. Also remember what I said about overloading your parallel processor machine by making your fact tables overly parallel. Unless you have more CPUs than concurrent users, you probably don't want parallel. I've been to too many sites with fewer than 32 CPUs using parallel and suffering. If you have less than 16 CPUs, forget parallel query, unless you only have two concurrent users.

Q: What about fact table bitmap indexes and low cardinality?

This is my biggest data warehousing pet peeve question to date. Again, people are reading blanket Oracle documentation and not seeing what's being said. According to Oracle: "The advantages of using bitmap indexes are greatest for low cardinality columns in which the number of distinct values is small compared with the number of rows in the table." Most people seem to ignore the phrase "compared with the number of rows in the table." If the POS_DAY fact table has a billion rows and creates a bitmap index on PRODUCT_ID, that is low cardinality. Yes, PRODUCT has 200,000 rows. But that's small in comparison to a billion. Yet I get this question at least twice at every data warehousing presentation. (I'll cover bitmap index design for successful star transformation queries in much greater detail in a later section of this chapter.)

Q: We want to run a 24x7 data warehouse; how do we update bitmap indexes?

You can't. Bitmap indexes are a requirement for star transformation. And bitmap indexes do not update well; they generally corrupt and slow the load down by a factor of ten or more. I'll go back to Chapter 1 and ask: How can you require 24x7? A true data warehouse is for executives and senior managers; these guys work normal business hours of 9–5, and most are in the same location, headquarters. I've yet to meet anyone doing a truly strategic data warehouse and require more than 7x16. And I've talked to the DBAs of many Fortune 500 companies doing data warehouses.

Q: I cannot get star transformation explain plans. Why?

Simple; you did not adhere to the prerequisites. Remember, you cannot get a star transformation explain plan without proper INIT.ORA settings, bitmap indexes, and cost-based optimization (all of which will be covered in the next few sections). I've yet to find anyone whose star schema data warehouse is not a fit. Yet I hear people saying that their data is special and thus they cannot do star transformations. That's a lame excuse because nobody really has such specialized situations. It reminds me of programmers who blame compiler bugs every time their programs don't work.

INITIALIZATION PARAMETERS

The most common reason I find people having problems with star transformation explain plans is that they don't set the proper INIT.ORA parameters. In short, *if you don't have the proper initialization parameters set, you cannot obtain star transformation explain plans, even if you specify the STAR_TRANSFORMATION hint!* Please reread that last sentence again, possibly even twice, because 20% of the problem sites I visit have the simple problem of either not setting the right values or not setting them high enough.

For Oracle 8i, the following parameters must be set:

- ALWAYS_ANTI_JOIN = HASH
- ALWAYS_SEMI_JOIN = HASH
- BITMAP_MERGE_AREA_SIZE = 16MB or larger
- COMPATIBLE = 8.1.7
- CREATE_BITMAP_AREA_SIZE = 16MB or larger
- HASH_AREA_SIZE = 16MB or larger
- HASH_JOIN_ENABLED = TRUE
- OPTIMIZER_FEATURES_ENABLE = 8.1.7
- SORT_AREA_SIZE = 16MB or larger
- STAR_TRANSFORMATION = TRUE or TEMP_DISABLE

For Oracle 9i, the list is even shorter—just set the following parameters:

- BITMAP_MERGE_AREA_SIZE = 16MB or larger
- COMPATIBLE = 9.0.1 or 9.2.0
- CREATE_BITMAP_AREA_SIZE = 16MB or larger
- HASH_AREA_SIZE = 16MB or larger
- HASH_JOIN_ENABLED = TRUE
- OPTIMIZER_FEATURES_ENABLE = 9.0.1 or 9.2.0
- SORT_AREA_SIZE = 16MB or larger
- STAR_TRANSFORMATION = TRUE or TEMP_DISABLE

The STAR_TRANSFORMATION parameter is paramount here. Without it being set, there is absolutely no way to get a star transformation explain plan—not even by using the STAR_TRANNSFORMATION hint. This is the single most critical factor in getting the star transformation to work. Yet, 10% of the problem sites I visit have this simple problem. The default is FALSE, so please set this parameter.

One question that always comes up is what is TEMP_DISABLE and when or why should it be used? In Oracle 8.0, the STAR_TRANSFORMATION parameter was simply set to either TRUE or FALSE. However, beginning with Oracle 8i, the value of TEMP_DISABLE entered the mix, and in fact meant the same as TRUE in Oracle 8.0 (i.e., merely enabled), whereas TRUE now means both enabled and that Oracle can use temporary tables to store intermediate results. Specifically in the case where a dimension table may need to be accessed twice in the explain plan, the query optimizer may decide to create a temporary table for a subset of a dimension table instead of accessing that dimension table twice (e.g., when the dimension table is large and the selected subset seems to be small). Note that prior to Oracle 8.1.7.3, there were serious bugs with this optimization approach that could yield incorrect results or generate ORA-00600 errors.

The second most important initialization parameters to set are COMPATIBLE and OPTIMIZER_FEATURES_ENABLE. COMPATIBLE is often a problem because many people forget to change this parameter in their INIT.ORA file as they apply patches and/or install new versions. Likewise, the OPTIMIZER_FEATURES_ENABLE is just as important as it directly affects the behavior of the query optimizer (i.e., which optimizer features are in effect usable). Table 5–2 details the various optimizer features that are enabled by setting the different version settings:

Table 5–2   Oracle Version Support for Data Warehousing Features

Features	8.0.6	8.0.7	8.1.6	8.1.7	9.0.1	9.2.0
Index fast full scan	✔	✔	✔	✔	✔	✔
Consideration of bitmap access paths for tables with only b-tree indexes	✔	✔			✔	✔
Complex view merging	✔	✔			✔	✔
Push-join predicate	✔	✔			✔	✔
Ordered nested loop costing	✔	✔			✔	✔
Improved outer join cardinality calculation	✔	✔	✔	✔	✔	✔
Improved verification of NULLs inclusion in b-tree indexes			✔	✔	✔	✔
Random distribution method for left of nested loops			✔	✔	✔	✔
Type-dependent selectivity estimates			✔	✔	✔	✔
Setting of optimizer mode for user-recursive SQL			✔	✔	✔	✔
Improved average row length calculation			✔	✔	✔	✔
Partition pruning based on sub-query predicates			✔	✔	✔	✔
Common sub-expression elimination				✔	✔	✔
Use statistics of a column embedded in some selected functions such as TO_CHAR to compute selectivity				✔	✔	✔
Improved partition statistics aggregation				✔	✔	✔
Peeking at user-defined bind variables					✔	✔
Index joins					✔	✔
Sub-query un-nesting					✔	✔

The initialization parameters BITMAP_MERGE_AREA_SIZE and CREATE_BITMAP_AREA_SIZE affect explain plan bitmap merge operations and bitmap index creation, respectively. Remember that star transformation depends heavily on bitmap indexes, so these initialization parameters are quite important. Also, remember that these settings apply per Oracle process, so if you're using parallel DML or parallel query, factor the size times the number of processes against your total overall memory consumption calculations.

The initialization parameters HASH_AREA_SIZE and HASH_JOIN_ENABLED affect explain plan hash join operations and whether hash joins are enabled, respectively. Remember that star transformation depends heavily on hash joins, so these initialization parameters are quite important. Also, remember that these settings apply per Oracle process, so if you're using parallel DML or parallel query, factor the size times the number of processes against your total overall memory consumption calculations.

Finally, increasing the initialization parameter SORT_AREA_SIZE improves the efficiency of large sorts as they can be performed in memory rather than on-disk. The default is a scant 64K, which is far too small for a data warehouse. Also, remember that these settings apply per Oracle process, so if you're using parallel DML or parallel query, factor the size times the number of processes against your total overall memory consumption calculations.

STAR SCHEMA INDEX DESIGN

This is the section where most DBAs' eyes roll back and they begin to question these techniques with heated fervor. This section will discuss the bitmap index design required for getting star transformation explain plans. So without further adieu, let me give the recommendations and then try to explain exactly why it must be done this way:

- Create a separate bitmap index on each fact table's dimension table's foreign key columns
- Create a separate bitmap index on each non-key column in the dimension tables

That does not sound too bad, until you think a little more about it. What I am saying is that you fully index your dimension table columns using bitmap indexes, and that you also create bitmap indexes on your fact table columns that refer back to your dimension tables. Let's return to our star schema data model from Chapter 4 and demonstrate what this means. Look at the star schema data model shown in Figure 5–6. I've placed an arrow next to each column that should get its own bitmap index.

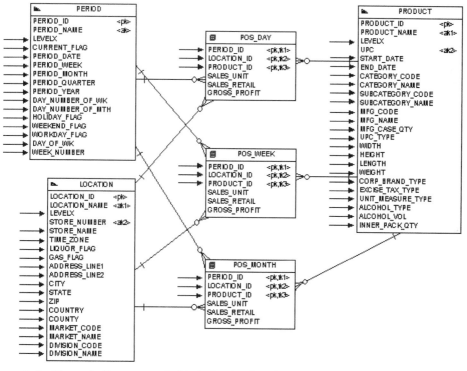

Figure 5–6   Example Recommended Indexing for Star Schema Design

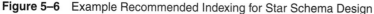

To summarize Figure 5–6, there are:

- 3 dimension tables
- 3 fact tables
- 77 total columns
- 11 b-tree indexes (for pks and aks)
- 60 bitmap indexes

That's a total of 71 indexes out of 77 columns! That's one heck of a lot of indexes.

So which of these indexes, if any, are superfluous? Well if you knew that, your ETL data loaders would never try to load duplicate records, and both primary and unique indexes would not be necessary. They are only there to keep the data clean. You never want to see any of these b-tree indexes in an explain plan or queries will run slowly. For a successful star transformation, you only want to see bitmap indexes in the explain plan, period.

I usually get three index-specific questions:

Q: What about fact table bitmap indexes and low cardinality?

This is my biggest data warehousing pet peeve question to date. Again, it is a case of people reading blanket Oracle documentation and not seeing what's being said. According to Oracle: "The advantages of using bitmap indexes are greatest for low cardinality columns in which the number of distinct values is small compared with the number of rows in the table." Most people seem to ignore the phrase "compared with the number of rows in the table." If the POS_DAY fact table has a billion rows and creates a bitmap index on PRODUCT_ID, that is low cardinality. Yes, PRODUCT has 200,000 rows. But that's small in comparison to a billion.

Q: Why index all the dimension columns?

Remember, dimension tables provide your ad-hoc end-users their WHERE clause column restriction selections. They are free to pick anything from that domain. You could try and index just those you thought were most likely to be selected, but you'd find that within a month or so, you'd have them all indexed anyhow. Why? Remember that I said you could judge your warehouse's success with one simple question: Do your users run more reports than they initially expected? If your data warehouse runs reports quickly, business users will drill deeper into "what-if" scenarios and do more than they ever planned. And if they do more, then eventually they'll utilize most if not all the dimension columns as WHERE clause criteria. So why not just index them all from Day One and thereby avoid the whole issue altogether?

Q: Why not use b-tree indexes for some dimension columns based on their data type?

Look back at Figure 5–6. The LOCATION dimension has columns MARKET_NAME and DIVISION_NAME, which are both
character, rather lengthy in size, and thus can have lots of unique values. Why not create b-tree indexes on these instead of bitmap
indexes? The answer is simple: Star transformation uses bitmap
indexes. If you make these b-trees, then the optimizer will add a step
at runtime (for each query) to convert the b-tree index to a bitmap
index so that it can be used by the star transformation. So why do that
runtime conversion for every query? Why not just make it a bitmap
and forgo the runtime conversion?

Note that I've included a handy script (below) for creating all
these bitmap indexes on your dimension tables. Run this in SQL Plus
using @FILE_NAME TABLE_NAME, where FILE_NAME is the
name of the script file and TABLE_NAME is the name of the dimension table that you want to fully bitmap index. It skips over columns
that are parts of either primary or unique keys and reverts to b-tree
indexes for numeric columns longer than NUM_SIZE or character columns greater than CHAR_SIZE. You can, of course, change the
DEFINE variables at the top of the script to suit your specific tastes.
Note too that this script actually writes another script (idx_dim.tmp)
to accomplish the task.

```
set define '&'

define num_size=20
define char_size=50

set echo off
set tab off
set heading off
set verify off
set feedback off
set pagesize 0
set linesize 256
set term off

spool idx_dim.tmp

select 'create '||
       decode(tc.data_type,
```

```
                    'DATE','         ',
                    'NUMBER',   decode(data_scale,
                                      0,decode(sign(&num_size-data_precision),
                                               -1,'        ',
                                               'bitmap'
                      ),
                                       '         '
                      ),
                    'CHAR',     decode(sign(&char_size-data_length),
                                       -1,'        ',
                                       'bitmap'
                                 ),
                    'VARCHAR2',decode(sign(&char_size-data_length),
                                       -1,'        ',
                                       'bitmap'
                                 ),
                      '         '
                )||
          ' index '||tc.table_name||
          decode(tc.data_type,
                    'DATE','_N',
                    'NUMBER',   decode(data_scale,
                                      0,decode(sign(&num_size-data_precision),
                                               -1,'_N',
                                               '_B'
                      ),
                                            '_N'
                      ),
                    'CHAR',     decode(sign(&char_size-data_length),
                                       -1,'_N',
                                       '_B'
                                 ),
                    'VARCHAR2',decode(sign(&char_size-data_length),
                                       -1,'_N',
                                       '_B'
                                 ),
                    '_N'
                )||
          decode(length(tc.column_id),1,'0',null)||to_char(tc.column_id)||
          ' on '||tc.table_name||'('||tc.column_name||')'
          pctfree 1 nologging;'
  from user_tab_columns tc
  where tc.table_name in upper('&1')
    and not exists (select 1
                    from user_cons_columns cc,
                         user_constraints co
                    where co.table_name = tc.table_name
                      and co.constraint_name = cc.constraint_name
```

```
                           and co.owner = cc.owner
                           and co.table_name = cc.table_name
                           and co.constraint_type in ('P','U')
                           and co.status = 'ENABLED'
                           and cc.column_name = tc.column_name
                       )
    and not exists (select 1
                       from user_ind_columns ic,
                            user_indexes ix
                      where ix.table_name = tc.table_name
                        and ix.index_name = ic.index_name
                        and ix.table_name = ic.table_name
                        and ix.status = 'VALID'
                        and ic.column_name = tc.column_name
                       )
order by tc.table_name, tc.column_id;

spool off

set term on
set heading on
set feedback on

@idx_dim.tmp
```

Finally, there is a little known Oracle table parameter to control the bitmap index creation algorithm. I say "little known" because you do not specify it on the create index command, but instead on the alter table command (prior to creating any bitmap indexes on that table) to control this behavior. The syntax is:

```
ALTER TABLE table_name MINIMIZE_RECORDS_PER_BLOCK
```

This tells Oracle to optimize the mapping of bitmaps to ROWIDs when creating any bitmap index on the table. You only want to do this when you know that the bitmap indexes will be fairly static, meaning not updated. Of course, in a data warehouse, this makes sense. And, setting it for your fact tables (and thus all their bitmap indexes) can save a fair amount of space.

COST-BASED OPTIMIZER

Star transformation requires the cost-based optimizer. That's all there is to it. Fortunately, the statistics collection method required is also quite simple. For both the dimensions and facts, simply run the following:

```
ANALYZE TABLE table_name ESTIMATE STATISTICS FOR TABLE FOR ALL INDEXES
FOR ALL INDEXED COLUMNS SAMPLE 20,000 ROWS
```

We run this command to accomplish two goals. First, we must provide the optimizer enough information so that it knows that star transformation is valid. Second, we must provide the optimizer enough information so that it knows absolutely never to utilize any b-tree indexes. You could even add histograms to your analysis via the SIZE parameter, but this would only assist with the latter goal (as bitmap indexes do not use histograms). Of course, you could gather statistics using the DBMS_STATS package instead of the ANALYZE command (often preferable since DBMS_STATS offers parallel analysis capabilities); but, the end results would be the same.

I've generally only received three questions regarding statistics:

Q: Why sample only 20,000 rows and not 5% or a million rows?

I've found that 20,000 rows will yield the same results (generally) as taking much larger samples. And, a 20,000-row sample will analyze rather quickly. Forget using percentages. For example, one percent of a billion rows is 10 million rows, and a serial analyze that size will run quite a long time. Plus, it will not yield any better results. So why analyze more than you need to? You can get star transformation with just 20,000 rows.

Q: Is it better to analyze by partition?

Yes. I would merely adjust the above command and do it for each partition. The reason is simple: If you analyze at the partition level, the optimizer should do a much better job of identifying correct partition eliminations in your star transformation explain plans. That's worth the additional cost to gather the statistics.

Q: How often should statistics be gathered?

That's easy: every time you load data. If you load data weekly, then gather statistics once per week. If daily, then do it daily. By keeping the sample size small, even multi-terabyte data warehouses can re-analyze all their tables in a very brief time.

SOME PARTING THOUGHTS

As you've read, it's not that hard to obtain star transformation explain plans, and thus, fast ad-hoc report runtimes. But, I still find a lot of people wanting to push for parallel query and partitioning as their "silver bullets" for optimal performance. As I've expressed in this chapter, a non-partitioned and non-parallel query star transformation explain plan will run nearly as fast as a partitioned and parallel queried one. I'm stressing this because far too often, people turn on all the bells and whistles at once and then fail to hit the mark. If you start out with less features turned on and obtain star transformation, then turning on additional features will make things faster, and you will retain nearly identical star transformation explain plans.

To prove this, I've included four additional figures that show that the same star transformation explain plan is obtained for same query, even though parallel and partitioning options are varied as follows:

- Non-parallel and non-partitioned (Figure 5–7)
- Non-parallel and range-partitioned (Figure 5–8)
- Parallel and non-partitioned (Figure 5–9)
- Parallel and range-partitioned (Figure 5–10)

Please note that the star transformation portion of the explain plan is highlighted on the left-hand side of each figure, and is identical. Only the right-hand side changes (which is also highlighted) regarding parallel operations for some steps or partition elimination as an additional step. So again, if you can just get the basic star transformation explain plan to work, you can make it even better with these additional Oracle features.

```
Operation                        | Name               | Rows | Bytes| Cost  | TQ  |IN-OUT| PQ Distrib | Pstart| Pstop |
-----------------------------------------------------------------------------------------------------------------------
SELECT STATEMENT                 |                    |   1  |  60  |  41   |     |      |            |       |       |
 TEMP TABLE TRANSFORMATION        |                    |      |      |       |     |      |            |       |       |
  RECURSIVE EXECUTION             | SYS_LE_2_0         |      |      |       |     |      |            |       |       |
   SORT GROUP BY                  |                    |   1  |  60  |  41   |     |      |            |       |       |
    HASH JOIN                     |                    |   1  |  60  |  29   |     |      |            |       |       |
     TABLE ACCESS BY INDEX ROWID  | POS_DAY            |  12  |  303 |  24   |     |      |            |       |       |
      BITMAP CONVERSION TO ROWIDS |                    |      |      |       |     |      |            |       |       |
       BITMAP AND                 |                    |      |      |       |     |      |            |       |       |
        BITMAP MERGE              |                    |      |      |       |     |      |            |       |       |
         BITMAP KEY ITERATION     |                    |      |      |       |     |      |            |       |       |
          TABLE ACCESS BY INDEX ROWID | PERIOD         |   1  |  51  |   2   |     |      |            |       |       |
           BITMAP CONVERSION TO ROWIDS |               |      |      |       |     |      |            |       |       |
            BITMAP AND            |                    |      |      |       |     |      |            |       |       |
             BITMAP INDEX SINGLE VALUE | PERIOD_B03    |      |      |       |     |      |            |       |       |
             BITMAP INDEX SINGLE VALUE | PERIOD_B07    |      |      |       |     |      |            |       |       |
          BITMAP INDEX RANGE SCAN | POS_DAY_B1         |      |      |       |     |      |            |       |       |
        BITMAP MERGE              |                    |      |      |       |     |      |            |       |       |
         BITMAP KEY ITERATION     |                    |      |      |       |     |      |            |       |       |
          TABLE ACCESS BY INDEX ROWID | LOCATION       |   1  |  46  |   2   |     |      |            |       |       |
           BITMAP CONVERSION TO ROWIDS |               |      |      |       |     |      |            |       |       |
            BITMAP AND            |                    |      |      |       |     |      |            |       |       |
             BITMAP INDEX SINGLE VALUE | LOCATION_B03  |      |      |       |     |      |            |       |       |
             BITMAP INDEX SINGLE VALUE | LOCATION_B11  |      |      |       |     |      |            |       |       |
          BITMAP INDEX RANGE SCAN | POS_DAY_B2         |      |      |       |     |      |            |       |       |
        BITMAP MERGE              |                    |      |      |       |     |      |            |       |       |
         BITMAP KEY ITERATION     |                    |      |      |       |     |      |            |       |       |
          TABLE ACCESS FULL       | SYS_TEMP_0FD9D660F_|   1  |  13  |   2   |     |      |            |       |       |
          BITMAP INDEX RANGE SCAN | POS_DAY_B3         |      |      |       |     |      |            |       |       |
     TABLE ACCESS FULL            | SYS_TEMP_0FD9D660F_|  17  |  578 |   2   |     |      |            |       |       |
 INSERT STATEMENT                 |                    |  17  |  782 |  13   |     |      |            |       |       |
  LOAD AS SELECT                  |                    |      |      |       |     |      |            |       |       |
   TABLE ACCESS BY INDEX ROWID    | PRODUCT            |  17  |  782 |  13   |     |      |            |       |       |
    BITMAP CONVERSION TO ROWIDS   |                    |      |      |       |     |      |            |       |       |
     BITMAP AND                   |                    |      |      |       |     |      |            |       |       |
      BITMAP OR                   |                    |      |      |       |     |      |            |       |       |
       BITMAP INDEX SINGLE VALUE  | PRODUCT_B08        |      |      |       |     |      |            |       |       |
       BITMAP INDEX SINGLE VALUE  | PRODUCT_B08        |      |      |       |     |      |            |       |       |
      BITMAP INDEX SINGLE VALUE   | PRODUCT_B03        |      |      |       |     |      |            |       |       |
-----------------------------------------------------------------------------------------------------------------------
```

Figure 5–7   Star Transformation for Non-Parallel and Non-Partitioned

```
-----------------------------------------------------------------------------------------------------------------------
| Operation                       | Name               | Rows | Bytes| Cost  | TQ  |IN-OUT| PQ Distrib | Pstart| Pstop |
-----------------------------------------------------------------------------------------------------------------------
| SELECT STATEMENT                 |                    |   1  |  60  |  50   |     |      |            |       |       |
|  TEMP TABLE TRANSFORMATION        |                    |      |      |       |     |      |            |       |       |
|   RECURSIVE EXECUTION             | SYS_LE_2_0         |      |      |       |     |      |            |       |       |
|    SORT GROUP BY                  |                    |   1  |  60  |  50   |     |      |            |       |       |
|     HASH JOIN                     |                    |   1  |  60  |  38   |     |      |            |       |       |
|      PARTITION RANGE ITERATOR     |                    |      |      |       |     |      |            | KEY   | KEY   |
|       TABLE ACCESS BY LOCAL INDEX ROWID| POS_DAY_RNG  |   5  |  125 |  33   |     |      |            | KEY   | KEY   |
|        BITMAP CONVERSION TO ROWIDS |                    |      |      |       |     |      |            |       |       |
|         BITMAP AND                |                    |      |      |       |     |      |            |       |       |
|          BITMAP MERGE             |                    |      |      |       |     |      |            |       |       |
|           BITMAP KEY ITERATION    |                    |      |      |       |     |      |            |       |       |
|            BUFFER SORT            |                    |      |      |       |     |      |            |       |       |
|             TABLE ACCESS BY INDEX ROWID| PERIOD        |   1  |  51  |   2   |     |      |            |       |       |
|              BITMAP CONVERSION TO ROWIDS|              |      |      |       |     |      |            |       |       |
|               BITMAP AND          |                    |      |      |       |     |      |            |       |       |
|                BITMAP INDEX SINGLE VALU| PERIOD_B03    |      |      |       |     |      |            |       |       |
|                BITMAP INDEX SINGLE VALU| PERIOD_B07    |      |      |       |     |      |            |       |       |
|            BITMAP INDEX RANGE SCAN| POS_DAY_RNG_B1     |      |      |       |     |      |            | KEY   | KEY   |
|          BITMAP MERGE             |                    |      |      |       |     |      |            |       |       |
|           BITMAP KEY ITERATION    |                    |      |      |       |     |      |            |       |       |
|            BUFFER SORT            |                    |      |      |       |     |      |            |       |       |
|             TABLE ACCESS BY INDEX ROWID| LOCATION      |   1  |  46  |   2   |     |      |            |       |       |
|              BITMAP CONVERSION TO ROWIDS|              |      |      |       |     |      |            |       |       |
|               BITMAP AND          |                    |      |      |       |     |      |            |       |       |
|                BITMAP INDEX SINGLE VALU| LOCATION_B03  |      |      |       |     |      |            |       |       |
|                BITMAP INDEX SINGLE VALU| LOCATION_B11  |      |      |       |     |      |            |       |       |
|            BITMAP INDEX RANGE SCAN| POS_DAY_RNG_B2     |      |      |       |     |      |            | KEY   | KEY   |
|          BITMAP MERGE             |                    |      |      |       |     |      |            |       |       |
|           BITMAP KEY ITERATION    |                    |      |      |       |     |      |            |       |       |
|            BUFFER SORT            |                    |      |      |       |     |      |            |       |       |
|             TABLE ACCESS FULL     | SYS_TEMP_0FD9D6611_|   1  |  13  |   2   |     |      |            |       |       |
|             BITMAP INDEX RANGE SCAN| POS_DAY_RNG_B3    |      |      |       |     |      |            | KEY   | KEY   |
|      TABLE ACCESS FULL            | SYS_TEMP_0FD9D6611_|  17  |  578 |   2   |     |      |            |       |       |
| INSERT STATEMENT                 |                    |  17  |  782 |  13   |     |      |            |       |       |
|  LOAD AS SELECT                  |                    |      |      |       |     |      |            |       |       |
|   TABLE ACCESS BY INDEX ROWID    | PRODUCT            |  17  |  782 |  13   |     |      |            |       |       |
|    BITMAP CONVERSION TO ROWIDS   |                    |      |      |       |     |      |            |       |       |
|     BITMAP AND                   |                    |      |      |       |     |      |            |       |       |
|      BITMAP OR                   |                    |      |      |       |     |      |            |       |       |
|       BITMAP INDEX SINGLE VALUE  | PRODUCT_B08        |      |      |       |     |      |            |       |       |
|       BITMAP INDEX SINGLE VALUE  | PRODUCT_B08        |      |      |       |     |      |            |       |       |
|       BITMAP INDEX SINGLE VALUE  | PRODUCT_B03        |      |      |       |     |      |            |       |       |
-----------------------------------------------------------------------------------------------------------------------
```

Figure 5–8   Star Transformation for Non-Parallel and Range-Partitioned

Operation	Name	Rows	Bytes	Cost	TQ	IN-OUT	PQ Distrib	Pstart	Pstop
SELECT STATEMENT		1	60	40					
TEMP TABLE TRANSFORMATION					3,02	PCWC			
RECURSIVE EXECUTION	SYS_LE_3_1								
SORT GROUP BY		1	60	40	3,02	P->S	QC (RANDOM)		
SORT GROUP BY		1	60	40	3,01	P->P	HASH		
HASH JOIN		1	60	26	3,01	PCWP			
TABLE ACCESS BY INDEX ROWID	POS_DAY	12	303	22	3,01	PCWP			
BITMAP CONVERSION TO ROWIDS					3,01	PCWP			
BITMAP AND					3,01	PCWP			
BITMAP MERGE					3,01	PCWP			
BITMAP KEY ITERATION					3,01	PCWP			
TABLE ACCESS BY INDEX ROWID	PERIOD	1	51	2	3,01	PCWP			
BITMAP CONVERSION TO ROWIDS					3,01	PCWP			
BITMAP AND					3,01	PCWP			
BITMAP INDEX SINGLE VALUE	PERIOD_B03				3,01	PCWP			
BITMAP INDEX SINGLE VALUE	PERIOD_B07				3,01	PCWP			
BITMAP INDEX RANGE SCAN	POS_DAY_B1				3,01	PCWP			
BITMAP MERGE					3,01	PCWP			
BITMAP KEY ITERATION					3,01	PCWP			
TABLE ACCESS FULL	SYS_TEMP_0FD9D6616_	1	13	2	3,01	PCWP			
BITMAP INDEX RANGE SCAN	POS_DAY_B2				3,01	PCWP			
BITMAP MERGE					3,01	PCWP			
BITMAP KEY ITERATION					3,01	PCWP			
TABLE ACCESS FULL	SYS_TEMP_0FD9D6615_	1	13	2	3,01	PCWP			
BITMAP INDEX RANGE SCAN	POS_DAY_B3				3,01	PCWP			
TABLE ACCESS FULL	SYS_TEMP_0FD9D6615_	17	578	1	3,00	P->P	BROADCAST		
RECURSIVE EXECUTION	SYS_LE_3_0								
INSERT STATEMENT		17	782	13					
LOAD AS SELECT									
TABLE ACCESS BY INDEX ROWID	PRODUCT	17	782	13					
BITMAP CONVERSION TO ROWIDS									
BITMAP AND									
BITMAP OR									
BITMAP INDEX SINGLE VALUE	PRODUCT_B08								
BITMAP INDEX SINGLE VALUE	PRODUCT_B08								
BITMAP INDEX SINGLE VALUE	PRODUCT_B03								
INSERT STATEMENT		1	46	2					
LOAD AS SELECT									
TABLE ACCESS BY INDEX ROWID	LOCATION	1	46	2					
BITMAP CONVERSION TO ROWIDS									
BITMAP AND									
BITMAP INDEX SINGLE VALUE	LOCATION_B03								
BITMAP INDEX SINGLE VALUE	LOCATION_B11								

Figure 5–9 Star Transformation for Parallel and Non-Partitioned

Operation	Name	Rows	Bytes	Cost	TQ	IN-OUT	PQ Distrib	Pstart	Pstop
SELECT STATEMENT		1	60	50					
TEMP TABLE TRANSFORMATION					4,02	PCWC			
RECURSIVE EXECUTION	SYS_LE_3_1								
SORT GROUP BY		1	60	50	4,02	P->S	QC (RANDOM)		
SORT GROUP BY		1	60	50	4,01	P->P	HASH		
HASH JOIN		1	60	36	4,01	PCWP			
PARTITION RANGE ITERATOR					4,01	PCWP		KEY	KEY
TABLE ACCESS BY LOCAL INDEX ROWID	POS_DAY_RNG	5	125	32	4,01	PCWP		KEY	KEY
BITMAP CONVERSION TO ROWIDS					4,01	PCWP			
BITMAP AND					4,01	PCWP			
BITMAP MERGE					4,01	PCWP			
BITMAP KEY ITERATION					4,01	PCWP			
BUFFER SORT					4,01	PCWP			
TABLE ACCESS BY INDEX ROWID	PERIOD	1	51	2	4,01	PCWP			
BITMAP CONVERSION TO ROWI					4,01	PCWP			
BITMAP AND					4,01	PCWP			
BITMAP INDEX SINGLE VAL	PERIOD_B03				4,01	PCWP			
BITMAP INDEX SINGLE VAL	PERIOD_B07				4,01	PCWP			
BITMAP INDEX RANGE SCAN	POS_DAY_RNG_B1				4,01	PCWP		KEY	KEY
BITMAP MERGE					4,01	PCWP			
BITMAP KEY ITERATION					4,01	PCWP			
BUFFER SORT					4,01	PCWP			
TABLE ACCESS FULL	SYS_TEMP_0FD9D6618_	1	13	2	4,01	PCWP			
BITMAP INDEX RANGE SCAN	POS_DAY_RNG_B2				4,01	PCWP		KEY	KEY
BITMAP MERGE					4,01	PCWP			
BITMAP KEY ITERATION					4,01	PCWP			
BUFFER SORT					4,01	PCWP			
TABLE ACCESS FULL	SYS_TEMP_0FD9D6617_	1	13	2	4,01	PCWP			
BITMAP INDEX RANGE SCAN	POS_DAY_RNG_B3				4,01	PCWP		KEY	KEY
TABLE ACCESS FULL	SYS_TEMP_0FD9D6617_	17	578	1	4,00	P->P	BROADCAST		
RECURSIVE EXECUTION	SYS_LE_3_0								
INSERT STATEMENT		17	782	13					
LOAD AS SELECT									
TABLE ACCESS BY INDEX ROWID	PRODUCT	17	782	13					
BITMAP CONVERSION TO ROWIDS									
BITMAP AND									
BITMAP OR									
BITMAP INDEX SINGLE VALUE	PRODUCT_B08								
BITMAP INDEX SINGLE VALUE	PRODUCT_B08								
BITMAP INDEX SINGLE VALUE	PRODUCT_B03								
INSERT STATEMENT		1	46	2					
LOAD AS SELECT									
TABLE ACCESS BY INDEX ROWID	LOCATION	1	46	2					
BITMAP CONVERSION TO ROWIDS									
BITMAP AND									
BITMAP INDEX SINGLE VALUE	LOCATION_B03								
BITMAP INDEX SINGLE VALUE	LOCATION_B11								

Figure 5–10 Star Transformation for Parallel and Range-Partitioned

CHAPTER 6

Loading the Warehouse

Loading data should be the easiest part of data warehousing, right? Well, it's not. In fact, 90% of the problems in data warehouses for which I've been the production support DBA have been with the nightly batch cycles that load the data. In other words, when the beeper goes off at 2 a.m. four nights a week, it's usually because some data load batch job missed its "must start by" or "must complete by" time and therefore royally screwed up the remaining jobs for that cycle. The nightly paging was so bad on one project that my wife asked me to leave a perfectly good job because she needed her sleep (as it was affecting her job performance). Now that's serious!

So why is this true? Every developer who's ever worked with Oracle has had to load data at some point. And, loading data is not rocket science. But remember, we're talking about a data warehouse, where size does matter, and in a big way (no pun intended). A typical, non-aggregate fact table may require the loading of tens to hundreds of millions of rows per day. You cannot write inefficient data loading programs when dealing with that much raw data. But, the typical developer has not had to deal with such staggering sizing issues in his or her primarily OLTP-based experience. Furthermore, most Oracle developers tend to write record-oriented code (i.e., using cursors), which does not make effective use of multi-CPU machines. Hence, even very good developers generally produce inefficient data loading programs at first. Thus, the production support DBA often must educate and inspire them regarding the techniques in this chapter. The best method that I've found to date is to call the responsible developers every time you get paged at night, which seems to make the point both quickly and convincingly. Plus, it just feels darn good to share the pain.

Even after you have created efficient data loading programs, there is still one more reason that data loading will represent the majority of your production support problems: concurrent job mixture and dependencies. Often, finding just the right execution order for dependent jobs and job sets on your existing hardware for your permitted time schedule is like finding a needle in a haystack. It's not uncommon to hold regular team meetings just to review and modify batch job schedules based on the most recent execution experiences. And as your data warehouse adds new data load jobs over time, these meetings also provide an excellent forum and foundation during which to request hardware upgrades.

WHAT ABOUT ETL TOOLS?

I get asked about ETL tools at every single consulting and speaking engagement. To date, I've not used any ETL tool on any data warehouse. My reasons are simple:

- ETL tools generally do not produce optimally efficient code.
- ETL tools cost money—often more than the hours they replace.
- There are too darn many to choose from (see Table 6–1).

Of course, the ETL vendors will firmly dispute my first point; so be it. But, these vendors (even Oracle with their Warehouse Builder) are generally at least a year behind when it comes to supporting the latest database features for optimally efficient data loading. Remember that I've said several times throughout this book that you'll want to be on the bleeding edge of Oracle releases and patches so you can utilize and benefit from such new features. More importantly, the lack of such features may limit your data loading architecture implementation options (e.g., you may be forced into a multi-step loading process with intermediate staging tables). Thus, having an ETL tool at least a year behind the database features may limit your implementation options, and this defeats the purpose. And we're talking about loading massive amounts of data. I've benchmarked several of these ETL tools versus custom code. The closest competition was twice as slow as well-written custom code. And ETL tools with Java transform engines ran orders of magnitude slower. So, you're trading data loading speed for a pretty GUI and sub-optimal code generation, period.

As for cost, I mean much more than just the purchase price—although for some of these ETL tools, the price can reach hundreds of thousands of dollars. There are some very big hidden costs as well. Some ETL tools require your software architecture to conform to their deployment paradigm. I call this buying a square-pegged ETL tool to fit into the round hole of your ETL environment. For example, Oracle's Warehouse Builder generates TCL scripts for scheduling via Oracle's Enterprise Manager. Well, what if you don't use Oracle's Enterprise Manager or TCL? Ever try telling a production support center they had to adopt a new job scheduler? And how about training all your staff on a new language (in case they have to debug the generated code)? These are costs, and big ones at that. Is it really worth it for generating sub-optimal code? Therefore, it's all these hidden costs that make ETL tools a sketchy bet at best.

There's one other cost to ETL tools I'm hesitant to expose because it's going to offend some people—oh well, so be it. ETL tools permit staffing your data loading team with nearly anyone available to generate your ETL programs, regardless of their Oracle and data warehousing experience. It's bad enough that the Oracle field is littered with people who claim to be premier Oracle developers but don't know how to write basic SQL. For example, my all-time favorite is the senior developer with supposedly four plus years of Oracle experience walking into my cubicle and asking what the plus sign is for in a SELECT statement's WHERE clause. Many Oracle developers I've met don't know SQL basics such as sub-queries, correlated sub-queries, tree-walk queries (i.e., START WITH and CONNECT BY), exists, not exists, unions, minus, etc. Do you really want to give these people a code generator to hide behind? Most DBAs know exactly what I'm talking about here. "Garbage in, garbage out" only gets worse with code generators in the hands of weak developers. It very quickly becomes a little garbage in, a lot of garbage out, with the DBA left holding the bag.

Finally, there is the overwhelming multitude of ETL tools to choose from, as shown in Table 6–1.

Table 6–1   World of ETL Tools Available

ETL Product Name	Vendor
ActaWorks	Acta Technologies
Amadea	ISoft
ASG-XPATH	Allen Systems Group
AT Sigma W-Import	Advanced Technologies
AutoImport	White Crane Systems
Automatic Data Warehouse Builder	Gilbert Babin
Blue Data Miner	Blue Data
Catalyst	Synectics Solutions
CDB/Superload	CDB Software
Cerebellum Portal Integrator	Cerebellum Software
Checkmate	BitbyBit International Ltd.
Chyfo	Ispirer Systems
CMS TextMap	Cornerstone Management Systems
Compleo	Symtrax
Content Connect	One Page
Convert /IDMS-DB, Convert/VSAM	Forecross Corporation
Conversions Plus	DataViz
Copy Manager	Information Builders, Inc.
CoSORT	Innovative Routines International, Inc.
CrossXpress	Cross Access Corporation
Cubeware Importer	CubeWare
Cyklop	Tokab Software AB
Data Cycle	APE Software Components S.L.
Data Exchange	XSB
Data EXTRactor	DogHouse Enterprises
Data Flow Manager	Peter's Software
Data Junction, Content Extractor	Data Junction
Data Manager	Joe Spanicek
Data Mapper	Applied Database Technology
Data Migration Tools	Friedman & Associates
Data Migrator for SAP, PeopleSoft	Information Builders, Inc.
Data Propagation System	Treehouse Software
Data Warehouse Tools	Javacorporate
Data[3]	Inform Information Systems

Table 6–1   World of ETL Tools Available (Continued)

ETL Product Name	Vendor
DataBlaster 2	Bus-Tech, Inc.
DataBrix Data Manager	Lakeview Technology
DataConvert	Metadata Information Partners
DataDigger	Donnell Systems
DataExchanger SRV	CrossDataBase Technology
Datagration	Paladyne
DataImport	Spalding Software
DataLoad	Software Technologies Corporation
DataManager	Joe Spanicek
DataMIG	Dulcian, Inc.
DataMiner	Placer Group
DataMirror Constellar Hub	DataMirror Corporation
DataMirror Transformation Server	DataMirror Corporation
DataProF	IT Consultancy Group BV
DataPropagator	IBM
DataProvider	Order Software Company
DataPump for SAP R/3	Transcope AG
DataStage XE	Ascential Software
DataSuite	Pathlight Data Systems
Datawhere	Miab Systems Ltd.
DataX	Data Migrators
DataXPress	EPIQ Systems
DB/Access	Datastructure
DBMS/Copy	Conceptual Software, Inc.
DBridge	Software Conversion House
DEAP I	DEAP Systems
DecisionBase	Computer Associates
DecisionStream	Cognos
DECISIVE Advantage	InfoSAGE, Inc.
Departmental Suite 2000	Analytical Tools Inc.
DETAIL	Striva Technology
Distribution Agent for MVS	Sybase
DocuAnalyzer	Mobius Management
DQtransform	Metagon Technologies
DT/Studio	Embarcadero Technologies

Table 6–1   World of ETL Tools Available (Continued)

ETL Product Name	Vendor
DTS	Microsoft
e-Sense Gather	Vigil Technologies
e-zMigrate	e-zdata.net
eIntegration Suite	Taviz Technology
Environment Manager	WhiteLight Technology
ETI Extract	Evolutionary Technologies, Inc.
ETL Engine	FireSprout
ETL Manager	iWay Software
eWorker Portal, eWorker Legacy	entrinsic.com
EZ-Pickin's	ExcelSystems
FastCopy	SoftLink
File-AID/Express	CompuWare
FileSpeed	Computer Network Technology
Formware	Captiva Software
FOXTROT	EnableSoft, Inc.
Fusion FTMS	Proginet
Gate/1	Selesta
Génio	Hummingbird Communications Ltd.
Gladstone Conversion Package	Gladstone Computer Services
GoHunter	Gordian Data
Graphical Performance Series	Vanguard Solutions
Harvester	Object Technology UK
HIREL	SWS Software Services
iManageData	BioComp Systems
iMergence	iMergence Technologies
InfluX	Network Software Associates, Inc.
InfoLink/400	Batcom
InfoManager	InfoManager Oy
InfoRefiner, InfoTransport, InfoHub, InfoPump	Computer Associates
Information Discovery Platform	Cymfony
Information Logistics Network	D2K
InformEnt	Fiserv
InfoScanner	WisoSoftCom
InScribe	Critical Path
InTouch/2000	Blue Isle Software, Inc.

Table 6–1   World of ETL Tools Available (Continued)

ETL Product Name	Vendor
ISIE	Artaud, Courthéoux & Associés
John Henry	Acme Software
KM.Studio	Knowmadic
LiveTransfer	Intellicorp
LOADPLUS	BMC Software
Mainframe Data Engine	Flatiron Solutions
Manheim	PowerShift
Mercator	TSI International
Meta Integration Works	Meta Integration Technologies
MetaSuite	Minerva Softcare
MetaTrans	Metagenix
MineWorks/400	Computer Professional Systems
MinePoint	MinePoint
MITS	Management Information Tools
Monarch	Datawatch Corporation
Mozart	Magma Solutions
mpower	Ab Initio
MRE	SolutionsIQ
NatQuery	NatWorks, Inc
netConvert	The Workstation Group, Ltd.
NGS-IQ	New Generation Software
NSX Data Stager	NSX Software
ODBCFace	System Tech Consulting
OLAP Data Migrator	Legacy to Web Solutions
OmniReplicator	Lakeview Technology
OpalisRendezVous	Opalis
Open Exchange	IST
OpenMigrator	PrismTech
OpenWizard Professional	OpenData Systems
OptiLoad	Leveraged Solutions, Inc.
Oracle Warehouse Builder	Oracle Corporation
Orchestrate	Torrent Systems Inc.
Outbound	Firesign Computer Company
Parse-O-Matic	Pinnacle Software
ParseRat	Guy Software

Table 6–1   World of ETL Tools Available (Continued)

ETL Product Name	Vendor
pcMainframe	cfSOFTWARE
PinnPoint Plus	Pinnacle Decision Systems
PL/Loader	Hanlon Consulting
PointOut	mSE GmbH
Power*Loader Suite	SQL Power Group
PowerDesigner WarehouseArchitect	Powersoft
PowerMart	Informatica
PowerStage	Sybase
Rapid Data	Open Universal Software
Relational DataBridge	Liant Software Corporation
Relational Tools	Princeton Softech
ReTarGet	Tominy
Rodin	Coglin Mill Pty Ltd.
Roll-Up	Ironbridge Software
Sagent Solution	Sagent Technology, Inc.
SAS/Warehouse Adminstrator	SAS Institute
Schemer Advanced	Appligator.com
Scribe Integrate	Scribe Software Corporation
Scriptoria	Bunker Hill
SERdistiller	SER Solutions
Signiant	Signiant
SpeedLoader	Benchmark Consulting
SPINA PRO	Diagnos
SRTransport	Schema Research Corp.
StarQuest Data Replicator	StarQuest Software
StarTools	StarQuest
Stat/Transfer	Circle Systems
Strategy	SPSS
Sunopsis	Sunopsis
SyncSort Unix	Syncsort
TableTrans	PPD Informatics
Text Agent	Tasc, Inc.
TextPipe	Crystal Software Australia
TextProc2000	LVRA
Textractor	Textkernel

Table 6–1 World of ETL Tools Available (Continued)

ETL Product Name	Vendor
Tilion	Tilion
Transporter Fountain	Digital Fountain
TransportIT	Computer Associates
ViewShark	infoShark
Vignette Business Integration Studio	Vignette
Visual Warehouse	IBM
Volantia	Volantia
vTag Web	Connotate Technologies
Waha	Beacon Information Technology
Warehouse	Taurus Software
Warehouse Executive	Ardent Software
Warehouse Plus	eNVy Systems
Warehouse Workbench	systemfabrik
Web Automation	webMethods
Web Data Kit	LOTONtech
Web Mining	Blossom Software
Web Replicator	Media Consulting
WebQL	Caesius Software
WhizBang! Extraction Library	WhizBang! Labs
Wizport	Turning Point
Xentis	GrayMatter Software Corporation

LOADING ARCHITECTURE

Back in Chapter 2, we identified some key software architectural decisions the DBA must make. Principal among those were how many instances will comprise the data warehouse and will the data warehouse data be loaded in one step or two? In this chapter, we will focus on just the latter issue—loading the data.

When loading data into a data warehouse, there are two options (shown in Figure 6–1):

- Option 1—Load the data from the source directly into the data warehouse's query tables.

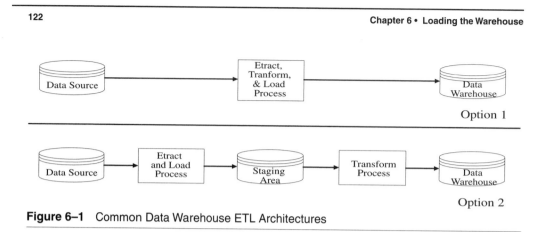

Figure 6–1   Common Data Warehouse ETL Architectures

- Option 2—Load the data from the source into a staging area first, then into the query tables.

We'll refer to these approaches as transform, then load and load, then transform, respectively. We reviewed the pros and cons of these approaches back in Chapter 2. Now, we'll examine optimally implementing them using Oracle 8i and 9i in the sections that follow. The implementation options are somewhat different since the database versions' features are different (i.e., newer Oracle versions tend to offer newer, better data warehousing solutions).

We also reviewed back in Chapter 2 that data loading programs must be designed to utilize SMP/MPP multi-CPU architectures, otherwise CPU usage may not exceed 1/No. of CPUs. The Golden Rules are very simple:

- Minimize inter-process wait states.
- Maximize total concurrent CPU usage.

Our goal will be to achieve a parallel loading architecture something like Figure 6–2.

However, we must first examine two other criteria before we can settle on our final data loading architecture: upstream data sources and data transformation requirements.

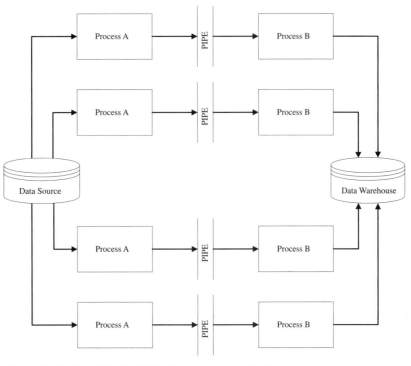

Figure 6–2   True Parallel ETL Processing via Forking

UPSTREAM SOURCE DATA

This is probably one of the easiest areas to explain. The majority of the time, your data warehouse source data will simply be files. Why files, you might ask, when all our applications are in relational databases? The reason is simple: 90% of the upstream OLTP application production support teams are not going to permit an external team (such as a data warehousing team) to write and schedule code to run against their production application. Why? Because if your code drags their system to its knees or blows apart their job schedule, then they get paged and will face any associated customer grief, not you. So they will provide you with files to meet whatever specifications you provide, but they will write the code and schedule it, not you. That's just how it's done in large shops with lots of controls.

Thus, we can adjust Figure 6–1 to look like Figure 6–3, where we removed the extraction concept and used data files as our data source. The approach names, transform, then load and load, then transform, probably now make more sense.

Of course there are exceptions to every rule. In some cases, you may be the DBA for both the OLTP and data warehouse applications. Or, your shop may not have as many controls. You might even have exceptional DBAs who coordinate their activities and share some of their responsibilities. If so, then you're very lucky. Every data warehouse I've worked on has been a separate team. As such, we've always had to document for other teams what output we needed from

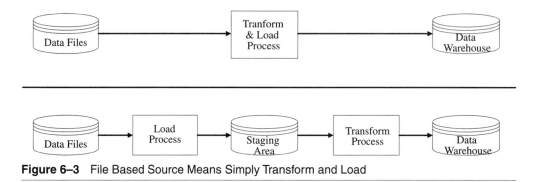

Figure 6–3   File Based Source Means Simply Transform and Load

their systems and then lived with whatever schedule they dictated for execution and delivery. Don't fret or fight it; it's just a normal control condition for successfully managing large-scale production applications.

The major problem you run into here is with scheduling. If the upstream applications cannot produce your necessary source data in time for you to process it before your data warehouse must come online, then you may have to process that data a day late. In other words, your data warehouse may be 24–48 hours behind the production OLTP systems' data. Take time to clearly explain this to the business sponsor; it should not be an issue. Remember, the data warehouse is used for strategic purposes, and a day or two behind should not impact truly long-term or strategic reporting/planning.

However, if the sponsoring user won't budge, then you'll have to open the warehouse later (i.e., whenever you can complete the data loads for the source data that arrives the latest). It may even be that you open portions of the warehouse at different times based on this. For example, order data may come online in the warehouse at 7:00 a.m., while sales data may not come online until 9:00 a.m. I've even done data warehouses where the data is always online, but is switched over to the most current day's load at 9:00 a.m. This lets the users do work, but they know that they will not have the previous day's data available until 9:00 a.m. The point is to be creative; when you get down to it, a data warehouse is really nothing more than a glorified reporting system. While it might be important to both high-level managers and executives, the organization can still book business via its OLTP systems. But, these people should be flexible when it comes to providing a platform from which to make truly strategic decisions.

I'm going to present the various data loading architecture implementations assuming a data source of files. The translation for these example implementations to instead use database tables as their data source (which should be quite simple and straightforward) is left to the reader as an exercise.

TRANSFORMATION REQUIREMENTS

Before we look at the implementation methods, it's key to understand the transformation process requirements as they directly affect the options available. In general, I have seen only three data transformation scenarios:

- Source data is already transformed (i.e., no transformation required).
- Source data requires very simple transformation operations.
- Source data requires very complex transformation operations.

The first and second scenarios almost never occur. If they do, then either you're really building an ODS—and hence this book's techniques generally do not apply—or somehow you've tricked the upstream application teams into producing your source data files with all your data transformations already complete.

Almost always, I find the third scenario to be the case. By more complex transformations, I mean data transformation operations more complex than simply:

- Substituting constants.
- Converting data types.
- Applying format masks.
- Assigning fields to a sequence number.
- Setting to NULL based on a condition.
- Setting a DEFAULT based on a condition.
- Using simple SQL operators (e.g., UPPER, TRUNC, SUBSTR, etc.).

You may recognize these data transformation operations as those available from within Oracle's SQL Loader. So another way to state the third scenario would be that your data transformation process requires logic more complex than that provided by SQL Loader.

For some data warehouses, another key data transformation requirement is the ability to update previously inserted data. I've always referred to this as doing an "UPSERT" (i.e., the combination of an UPDATE and an INSERT). Beginning with Oracle 9i, the new MERGE command directly supports this key data transformation need. However, the MERGE is only supported in SQL DML commands, not in Oracle's SQL Loader.

METHOD 1: TRANSFORM, THEN LOAD

Let me start by simply mapping out the optimally efficient transform, then load implementation options (shown in Figure 6–4).

Yes, there are implementation options other than those presented in Figure 6–4. But these methods represent the optimally efficient techniques available, period. Let's examine each of these five scenarios in more detail.

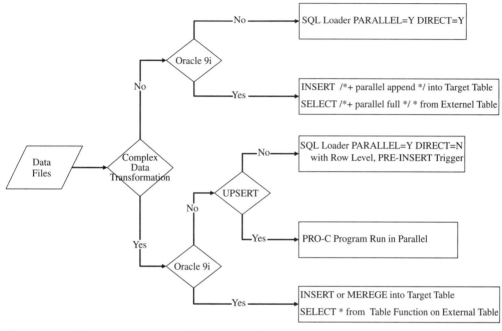

Figure 6–4 "Transform Then Load" Implementation Options

Scenario 1

If you only need simple data transformations and you're using Oracle 8i, then your best and most obvious choice is to simply use SQL Loader. Of course, you'll have to write the correct control file to implement your simple transformation logic, but otherwise, you can just run SQL Loader in parallel with direct mode load. There are, of course, two cases you may have to handle: many small, identical input files or one large input file.

Many small, identical input files is a natural fit for running SQL Loader in parallel with direct loads. It's really just a simple scripting exercise. Let's assume we're on a UNIX server, have 200 input files whose names start with xxx.inp, and that we want to execute 10 concurrent SQL Loader processes at a time until all 200 files are loaded. The UNIX shell script to accomplish this would be:

```
#!/bin/sh
degree=10
inp_name=xxx.inp
ctl_name=xxx.ctl
file_count=`ls -l ${inp_name}* | wc -l`
if [ $file_count ]
then
  rm -f file_list*
  ls ${inp_name}* > file_list
  split_count=`expr \( $file_count + $file_count % $degree \) / $degree`
  split -$split_count file_list file_list_
  for list in `ls file_list_*`
  do
    ( cat $list | while read file
      do
        if [ -s $file ]
        then
          sqlldr data=$file control=$ctl_name direct=true parallel=true
        fi
      done ) &
  done
  wait
fi
```

How does this script work? First, Line 9 creates a file that contains a list of the 200 filenames (in reality, the script would work for whatever number of files it finds). Second, Line 11 splits that complete list into a degree number of sub-lists, each containing *N*/degree number of filenames. So now we have 10 sub-lists each containing 20 filenames. Then, for each sub-list, Lines 14–20 create a parallel background process that loads each input file contained in that sub-list. Finally, Line 22 waits for all parallel threads to complete.

One large input file, on the other hand, is a bit more complicated to handle. It is most desirable to logically split the large file *N* ways, but preferably without having to increase the total I/O. For example, if we simply ran the UNIX split command on a large file to split it into smaller files, and then ran SQL Loader in parallel on those smaller files, we'd triple our I/O! Why? A split is essentially a copy (i.e., read and write of each record), and we would have to re-read the copied records. That's three times the I/O, and as any good DBA knows, I/O is the mortal enemy. Plus, we'd have to wait for the split to complete before starting any SQL Loader processing. So, we also would not be minimizing our inter-process waits. It does not get any worse than that—triple the I/O and fully maximized inter-process waits!

To avoid these performance issues, we will make extensive use of pipes. While it may sound like I'm splitting hairs here and that pipes are really no better than the split, they are. First, pipes are done in memory, so no additional I/O is incurred. Second, pipes reduce inter-process waits as they asynchronously connect processes. So, pipes are truly the way to go.

Let's assume that we're on a UNIX server, have one large input file whose name is yyy.inp, and that we want to execute 10 concurrent SQL Loader processes on that single file. The UNIX shell script to accomplish this would be:

```
#!/bin/sh
degree=10
inp_name=yyy.inp
ctl_name=yyy.ctl
tmp_name=/tmp/`basename $0`.tmp
if [ -s $inp_name ]
then
  i=0
  while [ $i -lt $degree ]
  do
    mkfifo pipe_a$i
    mkfifo pipe_b$i
    awk 'NR%4=='$i'{print $0}' < pipe_a$i > pipe_b$i &
    sqlldr data=pipe_b$i control=$ctl_name direct=true parallel=true &
    i=`expr $i + 1`
  done

  i=0
  j=`expr $degree - 1`
  x="cat $inp_name"
  while [ $i -lt $degree ]
  do
    if [ $i -eq $j ]
    then
      x="$x > pipe_a$i"
    else
      x="$x | tee pipe_a$i"
    fi
    i=`expr $i + 1`
  done

  echo $x > $tmp_name
```

```
sh $tmp_name
rm -f $tmp_name

i=0
while [ $i -lt $degree ]
do
   rm -f pipe_a$i
   rm -f pipe_b$i
   i=`expr $i + 1`
done
fi
```

How does this script work? For each desired parallel degree, the following occurs: First, Lines 10 and 11 create two named pipes: `pipe_a` and `pipe_b`. Second, Line 12 creates an `awk` record filter process in the background whose input is `pipe_a` and output is `pipe_b`. These `awk` filters permit us to have each parallel thread process a subset of the records based on the modulus from 0 to N-1 of the record numbers. Third, Line 13 creates a SQL Loader process in the background whose input is `pipe_b`. So, our overall parallel process flow looks something like:

pipe-a0 ➡ awk mod 0 filter ➡ pipeb0 ➡ SQL Loader
pipe_a1 ➡ awk mod 1 filter ➡ pipeb1 ➡ SQL Loader
...
pipea(N-1) ➡ awk mod N-1 filter ➡ pipe_b(N-1) ➡ SQL Loader

In Lines 17–29, we create a command string that we'll use to initiate the entire parallel processing architecture. What we want to do is `cat` the large file once and simultaneously feed that data to all the parallel process threads, which we do via unnamed pipes, the `tee` command, and output file redirection. Hence, the constructed command string will be of the form:

```
cat $inp_file | tee pipe_a0 | pipe_a1 | ... | pipe_a(N-2) > pipe_a(N-1)
```

Finally, we'll write that command string to a temporary file in Line 31 and execute it in Line 33. The reason we write it to a temporary file first and then execute it is that both the pipe and redirect characters in the command string can cause substitution problems for some of the various UNIX flavors if we merely try to execute that command string in place.

I'll leave it to the reader as an exercise to combine these two scripts for the case with lots of medium-sized files to load in parallel both across and within input files. Even if you decide not to try this exercise, think about it for a moment. Both the above scripts are not trivial, and combining them would take some effort. Remember this fact, because in later sections, where I say that new Oracle 9i features automate all the parallel implementation headaches for you, I mean as compared to these scripts and combining them. In Oracle 9i, you'll merely provide parallel DML and SQL hints to accomplish the exact same thing. That's why Oracle 9i is the way to go for data loading.

Scenario 2

If you only need simple data transformations and you're using Oracle 9i, then your best and most obvious choice is to use 9i's new external table mechanism. What exactly are external tables? Oracle defines them as the meta-data necessary to describe an external flat file such that Oracle can provide read-only access to that data as if it was a regular database table. Thus, Oracle abstracts away the implementation while providing the full expressive power of SQL, including parallel queries. Imagine, SQL for flat files!

As before, there are two cases you may have to handle: many small, identical input files or one large input file. This time, we'll look at these cases in reverse order since the one large input file case is now so simple as to be laughable.

Let's assume that once again, we're on a UNIX server, have one large input file whose name is yyy.inp, and that we want to execute 10 concurrent loading processes into our regular database table from that single external table (i.e., the input file). The Oracle 9i SQL code to accomplish this would be:

```
create directory inp_dir as '/home/oracle/input_files';

create table yyy (c1 number, c2 number, c3 number,
                  c4 number, c5 number, c6 number)
organization external (
    type oracle_loader
    default directory inp_dir
    access parameters (
        fields terminated by ','
```

```
    )
    location ('yyy.inp')
)
parallel 10;

alter session enable parallel dml;
insert /*+ parallel(fact,10) append */ into fact
    select /*+ parallel(yyy,10) full(yyy)*/* from yyy;
```

How easy is that? All we had to do was give Oracle just a few simple hints to get all that parallel processing done for us. Note that this code would work just the same on a Windows NT server (or any other OS for that matter).

Look back at the previous scenario's one large input file case; it was nearly 50 lines of complex scripting code to achieve the same results as our `insert select` with hints. I rest my case.

Many small, identical input files, on the other hand, is slightly more complicated to handle. But as before, it's really just a simple scripting exercise. Let's assume we're on a UNIX server, have 200 input files whose names start with xxx.inp, and that we want to execute 10 concurrent loading processes until all 200 files are loaded into our regular database table from that single external table (i.e., the input file).

First, we must update the previous example's external table such that it processes 10 files at a time (i.e., we now have 10 files instead of one listed under 10 locations). This will cause Oracle to process all those files at once (per operation). That's all there is to it.

```
create directory inp_dir as '/home/oracle/input_files';

create table xxx (c1 number, c2 number, c3 number,
                  c4 number, c5 number, c6 number)
organization external (
    type oracle_loader
    default directory inp_dir
    access parameters (
        fields terminated by ','

    )
    location ('file_0',
              'file_1',
              'file_2',
              'file_3',
```

```
                    'file_4',
                    'file_5',
                    'file_6',
                    'file_7',
                    'file_8',
                    'file_9')
)
parallel 10;
```

The UNIX shell script to process through all the input files would simply be:

```
#!/bin/sh
degree=10
inp_name=xxx.inp
ctl_name=xxx.ctl
file_count=`ls -l ${inp_name}* | wc -l`
if [ $file_count ]
then
  rm -f file_list*
  ls ${inp_name}* > file_list
  split_count=$degree
  split -$split_count file_list file_list_
  for list in `ls file_list_*`
  do
    i=0
    cat $list | while read file
    do
      rm -f file_$i
      ln -s $file file_$i
      i=`expr $i + 1`
    done
    sqlplus <<EOF
        alter session enable parallel dml;
        insert /*+ parallel(fact,10) append */ into fact
          select /*+ parallel(xxx,10) full(xxx)*/ from xxx;
EOF
  done
fi
```

How does this script work? First, Line 9 creates a file that contains a list of the 200 filenames (in reality, the script would work for whatever number of files it finds). Second, Line 11 splits that complete list into N number of sub-lists, each containing just a degree number of filenames. So now we have 20 sub-lists, each containing 10 filenames. Then, for each sub-list, Lines 15–20 create a soft link for each input file contained in a sub-list to location filenames for the external table (i.e., file_0 through file_*N*-1). Finally, Line 22 executes a SQL Plus session to load the files. This process repeats until all the file lists have been processed, and thus all the files have been loaded.

Scenario 3

If you need more complex data transformations, are only doing inserts (i.e., no updates), and you're using Oracle 8i, then your best choice is to use SQL Loader with row-level pre-insert triggers. Of course, you'll have to write the correct control file logic and trigger code to implement your data transformations, but otherwise, you just run SQL Loader in parallel without direct mode load (so the trigger can fire). In many respects, this scenario is very much like the first. In fact, you can use almost the exact same shell scripts, with the only modification being to change the lines calling SQL Loader from `direct=true` to `direct=false`—that's it.

Of course, you also need to create a row-level pre-insert trigger on the target table to perform your data transformation logic. An example would be:

```
create or replace trigger xxx_trg
before insert on xxx
referencing old as old new as new
for each row
declare
  av integer;
begin

  /* Obtain adjustment via lookup */
  begin
    select  adj_value
      into  av
      from  lookup_table
      where adj_lookup = :new.c2;
  exception
    when others then
      av := 0;
  end;

  /* Calculate final expression value */
  :new.c6 := nvl(:new.c4,0) + nvl(:new.c5,0) - av;

end;
/
```

In this example, we're calculating a column as an expression based on other columns from that same row and then applying adjustments to the calculated value based on some lookup table. Of course, our complex transformation logic is limited only by our PL/SQL coding ability. You cannot do this kind of stuff with just plain, old SQL Loader; you need the complete and expressive power of PL/SQL to accomplish such complex data transformations.

The reason this method only works for inserts (and not updates) is due to Oracle error ORA-04091: "Table schema.table is mutating, trigger/function may not see it." This error means: A trigger (or a user-defined PL/SQL function that is referenced in this statement) attempted to look at (or modify) a table that was in the middle of being modified by the statement that fired it.

Of course, the performance penalty for running SQL Loader with `direct = false` is somewhat noticeable. But, there really is no other way around this.

Scenario 4

If you need more complex data transformations, are doing upserts (i.e., updates that insert when a record is not found), and you're using Oracle 8i, then your best choice is to use Pro-C programs. Of course, you'll have to write the C code with embedded SQL to implement your data transformations. In many respects, this scenario is very much like both Scenarios 1 and 3. In fact, you can use almost the exact same shell scripts, with the only modification being to change the lines calling SQL Loader to instead call your Pro-C program. If that program is written to open files passed in as arguments, then the call would be of the form:

```
program_name file_name
```

But if the Pro-C program is instead just written to read from `stdio`, then the form would be:

```
cat file_name | program_name
```

Now, you might ask, why Pro-C instead of just using PL/SQL? That's a fair question. PL/SQL is a great language for doing database internal programming; plus now, with its supplied UTL_FILE package, PL/SQL can also operate on flat files. And, SQL Plus is a lightweight, command-line program that we could easily embed within our UNIX shell scripts (as we did in the multi-file case of Scenario 2) to execute our PL/SQL code. So again, why not just use PL/SQL?

Remember that my goal is to show you the most optimally efficient implementation, which is Pro-C. But for many shops, the answer will be to go with PL/SQL. The rationale is often that developers are more comfortable with PL/SQL (at least more so than with Pro-C and its associated makefiles). Plus, some UNIX vendors no longer provide a free C compiler (and Oracle currently only supports the GNU-C compiler on Linux). If that describes your shop, then by all means stick with PL/SQL.

PL/SQL lacks one key programming construct that Pro-C provides: Dynamic SQL Method #2: prepare and execute. This programming technique can shave about 15–20% off data loading program runtimes, so in many cases, it's worth the extra costs. How does this technique work? Remember, every time Oracle processes a command, it must parse, bind, execute, and fetch. With Dynamic SQL Method #2, you can prepare that statement once outside of your loop processing and then execute it repeatedly in the loop without Oracle having to re-parse or re-bind it.

As we did in Scenario 3, let's once again calculate a column as an expression based on other columns from that same row and then apply adjustments to the calculated value based on some lookup table. So, your Pro-C program would look like:

```
int main(int argc, char *argv[]) {
  ...

  strcpy(sql_command,"UPDATE xxx \
    SET c4 = nvl(c4,0) + nvl(:h_c4:i_c4,0), \
        C5 = nvl(c5,0) + nvl(:h_c5:i_c5,0), \
        C6 = nvl(c4,0) + nvl(:h_c4:i_c4,0) + \
             nvl(c5,0) + nvl(:h_c5:i_c5,0) - :h_av:i_av \
    WHERE c1 = :h_c1:i_c1 \
      AND c2 = :h_c2:i_c2 \
      AND c3 = :h_c3:i_c3;"
  EXEC SQL PREPARE update_command FROM :sql_command;

  strcpy(sql_command,"INSERT INTO xxx VALUES \
    (:h_c1:i_c1,:h_c2:i_c2,:h_c3:i_c3, \
     :h_c4:i_c4,:h_c5:i_c5, \
     nvl(:h_c4:i_c4,0) + nvl(:h_c5:i_c5,0) - :h_av:i_av)");
  EXEC SQL PREPARE insert_command FROM :sql_command;
```

```
/* Process data file records */
while (fgets (rec, sizeof rec, fid) != NULL) {
  ...

  /* Obtain adjustment via lookup */
  EXEC select  adj_value
         into   :h_av:i_av
         from   lookup_table
         where adj_lookup = :h_c2:i_c2;
  if (sqlca.sqlcode == 1403) {
    h_av = 0;
    i_av = 0;
  }
  else if (sqlca.sqlcode != 0) {
    ...
  }

  /* First - try to update existing record */
  EXEC SQL EXECUTE update_command
      USING :h_c1:i_c1,
            :h_c2:i_c2,
            :h_c3:i_c3,
            :h_c4:i_c4,
            :h_c5:i_c5,
            :h_av:i_av;

  /* Second - if update fails because record
              not found, then insert record*/
  if (sqlca.sqlcode == 1403) {
    EXEC SQL EXECUTE insert_command
      USING :h_c1:i_c1,
            :h_c2:i_c2,
            :h_c3:i_c3,
            :h_c4:i_c4,
            :h_c5:i_c5,
            :h_av:i_av;
  }
  else if (sqlca.sqlcode != 0) {
    ...
  }

  ...

}

...
}
```

Scenario 5

If you need more complex data transformations, you're possibly doing upserts (i.e., updates that insert when a record is not found), and you're using Oracle 9i, then your best choice is to use 9i's new external table mechanism and table functions, plus the new MERGE command if you're doing upserts. But let me state that while these new features represent the most optimally efficient ways to load data, they are far from the most obvious and easy ways to go. To effectively utilize these features, you as the DBA should assume a leadership and mentoring role for the developers. In short, these features leverage the database as the ETL engine, and as such, begin to blur the distinction between ETL developer and DBA.

If you're doing upserts, 9i's new MERGE command is simply a new DML command that encapsulates an UPDATE and INSERT into a single command processed by a single call to the database. Your developers will love this new syntax, as it's exactly what they've been coding as separate, related DML commands with intelligent error handling. Now it is a single command and a single network request sent to the database server. So you get the best of both worlds—it is easier to code and runs faster, too.

As for table functions, I like Oracle's definition: "A table function is defined as a function written in PL/SQL, Java, or C that can produce a set of rows as output and can take a set of rows as input." In essence, table functions sit between your source external table and final target table as ETL parallel piping mechanisms. Thus, Oracle now supports, via SQL, all the advanced parallel and pipelined ETL capabilities previously only available via shell scripts, Pro-C programs, and Oracle utilities.

Implementing Scenario 5 very closely resembles Scenario 2, but with two very minor exceptions. First, we can use either the INSERT or MERGE command. Second, we'll select our input data from a table function that is written against our external table. That's it. Let's dig deeper.

As before, there are two cases you may have to handle: many small, identical input files or one large input file. I'm only going to show the large file case. The reader should be able to very easily combine the example below with the one from Scenario 2 to produce the case for many small files.

Let's assume that once again we're on a UNIX server, have one large input file whose name is yyy.inp, and that we want to execute 10 concurrent loading processes into our regular database table from a single external table (i.e., the input file). And as with both Scenarios 3 and 4, we will calculate a column as an expression based on other columns from that same row and then apply adjustments to the calculated value based on some lookup table. Plus, like Scenario 4, we'll perform upserts. Whew. The Oracle 9i SQL code to accomplish this would be:

```
create directory inp_dir as '/home/oracle/input_files';

create table yyy (c1 number, c2 number, c3 number,
                  c4 number, c5 number, c6 number)
organization external (
    type oracle_loader
    default directory inp_dir
    access parameters (
        fields terminated by ','
    )
    location ('yyy.inp')
)
parallel 10;

create or replace type trx_obj is object (
  c1 number,
  c2 number,
  c3 number,
  c4 number,
  c5 number,
  c6 number,
  av integer
);
/
create or replace type trx_tab is table of trx_obj;
/

create or replace package trx
as
  type yyy_cur is ref cursor return yyy%rowtype;

  type trx_rec is record (
    c1 number,
    c2 number,
    c3 number,
```

```
    c4 number,
    c5 number,
    c6 number,
    av integer
  );
  type trx_tab is table of trx_rec;
  type trx_cur is ref cursor return trx_rec;


  function go (p yyy_cur)
    return trx_tab
    PIPELINED
    PARALLEL_ENABLE(PARTITION p BY ANY);
end;
/

create or replace package body trx
as
  function go (p yyy_cur)
    return trx_tab
    PIPELINED
    PARALLEL_ENABLE(PARTITION p BY ANY)
  is
    out_rec trx_cur;
  begin
    for inp_rec in p loop
      out_rec.c1 := inp_rec.c1;
      out_rec.c2 := inp_rec.c2;
      out_rec.c3 := inp_rec.c3;
      out_rec.c4 := inp_rec.c4;
      out_rec.c5 := inp_rec.c5;
      out_rec.c6 := inp_rec.c6;
      /* Obtain adjustment via lookup */
      begin
        select  adj_value
          into  out_rec.av
          from  lookup_table
          where adj_lookup = inp_rec.c2;
      exception
        when others then
          out_rec.av := 0;
      end;
      pipe row(out_rec);
    end loop;
  end;
end;
/
```

```
alter session enable parallel dml;
merge /*+ parallel(fact,10) append */
    into fact f
    using TABLE(trx.go(
        CURSOR(select /*+ parallel(yyy,10) full(yyy) */ *
                from yyy ))) y
    on f.c1 = y.c1 and
        f.c2 = y.c2 and
        f.c3 = y.c3
    when matched then
        update set
            c4 = nvl(f.c4,0) + nvl(y.c4),
            C5 = nvl(f.c5,0) + nvl(y.c5),
            C6 = nvl(f.c4,0) + nvl(y.c4) +
                nvl(f.c5,0) + nvl(y.c5) - y.av
    when not matched then
        insert values (y.c1, y.c2, y.c3,
                        y.c4, y.c5,
                        nvl(y.c4,0) + nvl(y.c5,0) - y.av);
```

We've now reached the point where the Oracle implementation is arguably as complex as the most involved shell scripting solution of any of the other scenarios. That's why the data warehouse DBA should be involved with ETL efforts when adopting this technique. Using the Oracle server as your ETL transformation engine like this is by far the fastest implementation choice there is. So, it's worth the extra effort to master this method.

METHOD 2: LOAD, THEN TRANSFORM

After the lengthy discussion regarding the transform, then load scenarios, a logical question is why would anyone choose load, then transform? There's really no great answer here that will universally justify this approach, but I can give some specific examples where I've seen it done, and with good reason in those particular instances.

If you need complex data transformations, you might decide to separate that logic from the basic data loading processes for developer resource allocation reasons. For example, you could have your junior team members write the loading jobs and your senior people write the complex data transformation jobs. By artificially separating these tasks, you can better allocate your developer resources. I've worked on projects where this was the case. It's a sound project management reason to adopt a load, then transform approach. I do, however, feel that Oracle 9i's advanced features make this less of an option than it was in the past. But, only you know your team's makeup and capabilities.

If you have a business requirement that your data loading jobs must be able to handle cumulative amounts of data, you might decide to separate the loading process from the data transformation logic so that you can still perform some work on those days when the loads are not promoted to your fact tables. Let me explain. Let's say that you have a nightly ETL process that updates your fact tables. However, on occasion (for legitimate business or technical reasons), you may need to collect the raw data for loading, but not promote that data to the fact tables until some later batch cycle run. Rather than just accumulating those files and having to process them all at once, it might be preferable to create a staging area in the database to accumulate that raw data. Then you could very easily perform just the transformation logic whenever it is permitted. This is probably the soundest reason I've seen for adopting a load, then transform approach.

But, the most common reason I run into is that the data warehouse was built before some of these features were available so the existing ETL code uses the historically popular choice of load, then transform. Moreover, new ETL jobs are written to conform to the exiting architecture, so the data warehouse does not evolve into a more modern approach. The guiding principal at these sites seems to be "If it ain't broke, don't fix it." They are more than content with this approach, and are willing to spend hardware dollars to stand pat. I even think some of these people would do it over the exact same way, meaning I'm not sure they know that other ways exist. For whatever reason, they're convinced that not only does it work, but it must be good since it was done that way. Unlike the previous two examples, I cannot say that this is a legitimate reason to adopt or maintain this approach.

So let's assume that for whatever reason, you are going to be working in a load, then transform paradigm; what are your implementation choices? For once, I have an easy answer. To load raw data into your staging tables, SQL Loader is the only way to go. It offers sufficient cleansing, trivial data transformations, performance, and ease of use as benefits to make all other choices irrelevant. And for promoting your staged data to your fact tables, SQL should be your first choice—with PL/SQL as your fallback. The architecture looks like Figure 6–5.

Figure 6–5   Using SQL Loader and PL/SQL to Load the Warehouse

The reason I say SQL first is for its set-oriented approach and parallel DML capabilities. Too often, developers fall into a PL/SQL rut of open cursor, loop though records till end of cursor, and perform operations on each record in the loop iteration. It reminds me of people doing file I/O programs, where they open file, read record, etc. You cannot load and transform tens to hundreds of millions of rows with such a limited and outdated programming approach. Compare the next two snippets of code:

```
-- SQL using parallel DML and direct mode loads
alter session enable parallel dml;
insert /*+ parallel(f,10) append */ into fact f
select /*+ parallel(s,10) full(s) */ * from staging_table s;


-- PL/SQL record-oriented cursor for loop
-- with a commit after every 100 records
commit_ctr := 0;
for rec in (select * from staging_table) loop
  insert into fact values (rec.c1, ... rec.cN);
  commit_ctr := commit_ctr + 1;
  if (commit_ctr >= 100) then
    commit_ctr := 0;
    commit;
  end if;
end loop;
```

The first snippet utilizes multiple CPUs and pushes both your CPU and I/O bandwidth consumptions to their limits. The second snippet uses one CPU and makes minimal resource requests overall. It just does not get it, so don't pick it.

So assuming that you have a legitimate reason to go this way, our optimally efficient load, then transform implementation options are (shown in Figure 6–6).

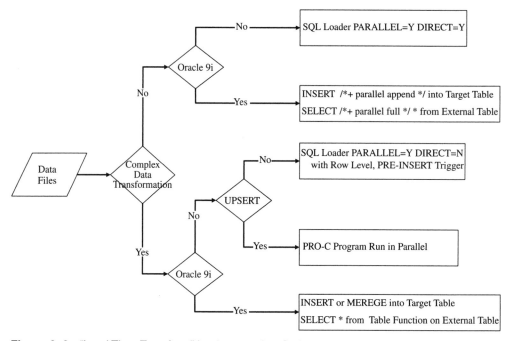

Figure 6–6   "Load Then Transform" Implementation Options

Looks a bit like Figure 6–4, which depicts our options for transform, then load, doesn't it? You should not be too surprised. On some of the choices, we merely had to change the word "External" to "Staging" (referring to the source table). Plus, all these approaches are entirely within the database (i.e., they copy data from one table to another). Most Oracle developers have little or no problems grasping such operations since they've been doing this kind of stuff since Day One. Of course it's this familiarity that too often has people choosing the load, then transform approach. I'm not going to detail the implementation choices in Figure 6–6 any further. The techniques are simple, and if you read the previous section, you already have code that is 90% of what you need for these implementation choices.

DEPLOYING THE LOADING ARCHITECTURE

The final step is to deploy your chosen data loading architecture, which means defining all its related tasks and their execution order. To some, this may seem intuitively obvious (e.g., dropping bitmap indexes before loading fact tables). But I've found it better to spell out the tasks involved to be sure.

For transform, then load, the tasks would be:

- Drop fact table bitmap indexes.
- Perform transform, then load.
- Create fact table bitmap indexes.
- Gather new fact table statistics.

For load, then transform, the tasks would be:

- Perform load (i.e., data files to staging table).
- Drop fact table bitmap indexes.
- Perform transform (i.e., staging table to fact table).
- Truncate staging table.
- Create fact table bitmap indexes.
- Gather new fact table statistics.

Note that we truncate the staging table only after a successful move of the staging data to the fact table. This permits us to perform cumulative batch cycle loads. Thus, we can stage any number of batch cycles' data before promoting that data to the fact table. If you remember, this was a key advantage of the load, then transform approach.

Implementing Aggregates

Aggregates are one of the key differentiators between successful data warehouses and otherwise mediocre attempts. As has been said several times throughout this book, successful data warehouses will experience much higher than originally expected end-user utilization, specifically more queries than planned. Why? Because if the data is easy to get at and the reports run quickly, the end-users will mine the data more than even they could have imagined. This will have another unexpected result: Your end-users will ask for more aggregate or summary tables as the data warehouse increases in size. Why? Because as the warehouse gets larger, they'll want you to maintain their fast report runtimes, and often, that will require creating aggregates. Of course, adding new tables will only serve to make the data warehouse grow even faster. So what? Disk space is cheap and happy end-users means job security.

What exactly is an aggregate? It is simply the rollup of an existing fact table along one of its dimensions, most often time. For example, if the base fact table is sales by day, then time-based aggregates might be sales by week, month, and quarter, with data volume reductions of approximately 1/7, 1/30, and 1/90, respectively. So, end-users doing trend analyses over somewhat long periods of time would benefit from querying smaller tables. Of course, as was said in Chapter 5, obtaining the correct explain plan is the most critical factor. But assuming the correct explain plan is being utilized, then querying a table that's 30 or 90 times smaller would only make a good thing much better. In real-world terms, a data warehouse fact table receiving 20 million rows each day and keeping 5 years of history online would contain 36 billion rows! However, the monthly aggregate would contain a more reasonable 1.2 billion rows, while the quarterly aggregate would contain a mere pittance of 400 million rows. With the right explain plan on just 400 million to 1.2 billion rows, end-user reports will run in seconds to minutes.

The DBA must be careful and manage the tradeoffs. With more aggregate tables come increased complexity, including disk space management, object management, partition management, and aggregate management. Of all these issues (and possibly others), the DBA must weight aggregate management the highest. Of course, there are the obvious aggregate issues, such as determining the calculation, creating the aggregate, updating the aggregate's values, and on occasion, reverifying the aggregate's data accuracy. But, it's the less obvious impact analysis that should be of more concern. For example, if you have a fact table that has six aggregates and you must change something regarding that fact table, it's possible that you'll invalidate one or more of the aggregates. And the problem may be much more than just breaking a calculation in a nightly summarization job. What if the fact change makes the contents of the existing aggregate invalid? You'd have to reassess and rebuild all the affected aggregates as well. Thus, aggregates are powerful weapons that must be researched and implemented with great insight.

WHAT AGGREGATES TO BUILD?

This is probably the simplest part of data warehousing, yet far too many DBAs make this much more of an issue than is necessary. Here are two simple rules to go by:

- Build whatever aggregates are required to make the end-users happy.
- Aggregates should be 10–100 times smaller than the fact tables on which they're based.

The first rule seems so simple, yet it's often the one where technical people have the most problems. Data warehouses are not traditional, normalized database designs. So then why argue with a business user over the technical merits of an aggregate? If they ask for it and it will be smaller than the fact it's based on, then just do it. The need for an aggregate is a business issue, not a technical question.

Another way to look at this is the importance of data warehouse end-users. These people are generally executives and senior managers from the business side. These people make business decisions at strategic and tactical levels. They're also the people who budget for internal support organizations, like IS. They don't just pay your salary, but run the company such that there is even a need for such support. In other words, these people make decisions such that the business prospers and grows. If the business doesn't prosper, there won't be any need for DBAs and data warehouses.

So if a business user is organizationally worthy of an aggregate, then just build it, even if that's the only person who will ever use it. For example, at 7-Eleven, beer represents a significant portion of both sales revenue and profit. So when the "beer" executive asked for an aggregate on daily sales related just to beer, we built it. Yes, there was a brief discussion on our development team about how all of our existing aggregates were based on time (e.g., week, month, quarter, year) and thus were generally useful to all end-users. But no one wanted say no to the beer guy—and rightfully so, he was the #3 person in the company.

The second rule also seems simple: Aggregates should be much smaller than what they summarize. The problem here is to make sure you find out from the businesspeople the information regarding the candidate fact tables. There is a belief on the technical side that all facts can be summarized equally well across the time dimension, but that's not true. Some facts may not summarize equally well across each of the time dimension's levels. For example, at 7-Eleven, the order fact had a billion rows and the order week aggregate had 650 million rows. How could this happen? The technical team's assumption was that all facts summarized at least to week and month, so those were the minimally, initially built aggregates. But the businesspeople knew that stores only order once per week and hence there was no need for an order week aggregate; the technical people never asked. So, the lesson here is: Don't guesstimate probable sizes for aggregates; ask the businesspeople.

Another way to create small aggregates is to build them on non-time dimensions. A typical time dimension with several hierarchical levels may still possess only a few thousand or tens of thousands of rows. Thus, aggregates based on time are based on domains of relatively small ranges and groupings within those domains. So, aggregating by month obviously only compresses to 1/30 of the original. And, aggregating by quarter compresses to 1/90 the original. Now, suppose you wanted to aggregate along a non-time dimension, such as products. For example, a typical retail store might have 400,000 distinct products, which represent 2,000 categories. Thus, you would have much larger domains and groupings within those domains on which to base aggregates, and aggregating by product category would compress to 1/200 the original.

Finally, don't hesitate to combine aggregation techniques. Returning to the "beer" example, why not build a beer aggregate by week, month, and quarter?

LOADING ARCHITECTURE

Remember, there are two data loading architectures for fact tables: transform, then load and load, then transform (see Figure 7–1).

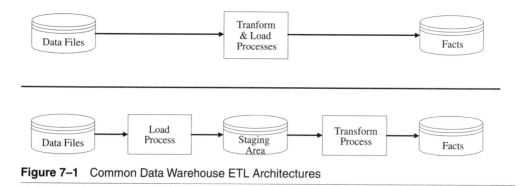

Figure 7–1   Common Data Warehouse ETL Architectures

The same data loading architecture options exist for loading aggregates; however, each of these scenarios becomes a bit more complex (Figures 7–2 and 7–3) as they add aggregation processes and aggregate tables to the flow. Plus, selecting an approach may limit your actual implementation options (e.g., does that approach work with materialized views?). You should review these options in detail and choose carefully.

The transform, then load architecture offers two options for including aggregates, as shown in Figure 7–2:

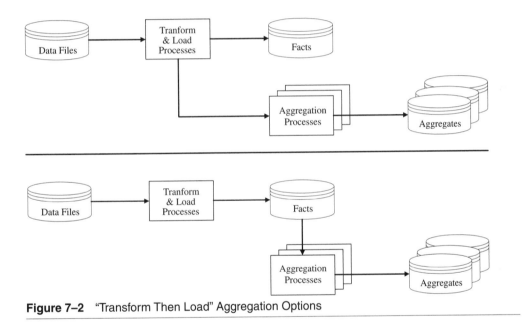

Figure 7–2 "Transform Then Load" Aggregation Options

The first option requires the transform and load program code to implement two distinct functions: the fact table transform and load, plus the aggregation for each aggregate. Although this can be accomplished via a single program that reads all the data once with no inter-process waits, that program will be significantly more complicated because it has to include logic for each target aggregate. This poses substantial project management risk as a single change to that one program could break the process for the fact and all its aggregates. Of course, you could implement each of the aggregate processes separately and feed them off the transform, then load approach via concurrent pipes, with commands like:

```
transform_then_load  |  tee aggregation_1  |  tee aggregation_2  …  >
aggregation_N
```

However, note this first option does not lend itself to a material-ized view implementation. While you could create the aggregates as materialized views and possibly utilize query rewrites, you would not be able to use the refresh mechanism, as refresh must be based on a table with a primary key. Even if the data files were accessed via external tables, you still could not do a refresh, as external tables also do not have primary keys. This is another drawback to this approach.

The second option separates the base fact and aggregate load logic. So, you don't have the project management nightmares related to having a single point of failure. In fact, you can implement each aggregation on its own, which is a natural fit for implementing via materialized views with refreshes (assuming that the aggregation pro-cesses will perform only inserts, as refresh does not yet support the MERGE command). This option also has the added benefit of subdivid-ing the tasks into more manageable and less complex pieces for developer resource allocation and batch job scheduling.

However, there are two drawbacks to this second option. First, you'll have to read the base fact table information at least twice (i.e., once to load it from the data files and a second time to summarize it). In fact, if you implement each of the aggregation processes sepa-rately, you'll then have to read the base fact table information $N+1$ times (where N represents the distinct number of aggregates based on that base fact table). Second, this option introduces an inter-process wait since you cannot load any of the aggregates until the fact has completed its data load. Nonetheless, you should view the second option as preferable to the first.

The load, then transform architecture also offers two options for including aggregates, as shown in Figure 7–3.

While Figure 7–3 may look fairly different than Figure 7–2, the two options are essentially the same, with nearly identical pros and cons. Either you have a complex program to read from the staging table into both the fact and its aggregates, or you have separate pro-grams for each. And, either you read the staging data once or once per aggregate. The only difference is that here with the first option, if you're using Oracle 9i, you could use parallel, pipelined table functions to implement the aggregations concurrently with the transform process. Refer back to Chapter 6 for an example of how to do this.

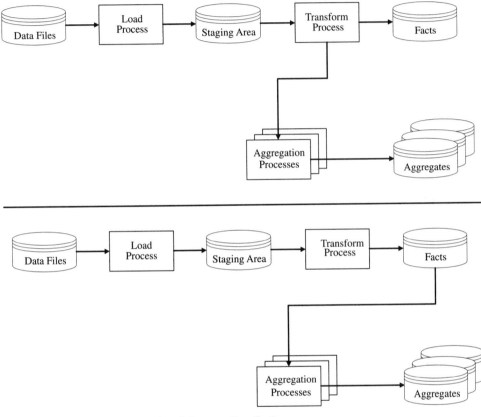

Figure 7–3 "Load Then Transform" Aggregation Options

Note that this approach is very complex and will require the DBA to stay intimately involved with the ETL process—probably more so than he or she may desire.

Once again, you should view the second option as preferable to the first.

AGGREGATION BY ITSELF

Now that all your options have been clearly spelled out, the reality is that there is really only one choice. Do not treat the aggregation process as part of the fact table data loading process (that's exactly why they're separate chapters in this book). Simply treat aggregation as its own distinct phase in the overall process (i.e., data load, then aggregate), as shown in Figure 7–4

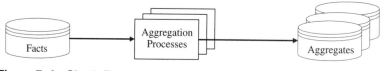

Figure 7–4   Simply Treat Aggregation Process by Itself

The astute observer will recognize that this was exactly what was being shown by a portion of the second option in both Figures 7–2 and 7–3. Look back and you'll see that by simply removing the data loading portion of the second option in both of these previous figures, all you're left with is exactly what's shown in Figure 7–4. This is, hands-down, the absolute best way to go.

The architecture separates the base fact and aggregate load logic. So, you don't have the project management nightmares related to having a single point of failure. In fact, you can implement each aggregation on its own, which is a natural fit for implementing via materialized views with refreshes (assuming that the aggregation processes will perform only inserts, as refresh does not yet support the MERGE command). This option also has the added benefit of subdividing the tasks into more manageable and less complex pieces for developer resource allocation and batch job scheduling.

However, there are two drawbacks to this option. First, you'll have to read the base fact table information at least twice (i.e., once to load it from the data files and a second time to summarize it). In fact, if you implement each of the aggregation processes separately, you'll then have to read the base fact table information $N+1$ times (where N represents the distinct number of aggregates based on that base fact table). Second, this option introduces an inter-process wait since you cannot load any of the aggregates until the fact has completed its data load.

A reasonable question that people often ask is: Why can't some of the aggregates be based off other aggregates with this approach? In other words, why can't the monthly aggregate be summarized from the weekly aggregate? In theory, it could. But recall the example where the week aggregate was found to be essentially useless? You'd have to rewrite the dependent aggregation process if the aggregate it's based on changed or became invalid. So why introduce unnecessary dependencies? Plus, you'd be introducing an inter-process wait state per dependency (e.g., you could not aggregate for month until week was complete). Always summarize from the base fact.

Mapping the optimally efficient aggregation processing options for various Oracle versions and summarization requirements yields the three scenarios shown in Figure 7–5

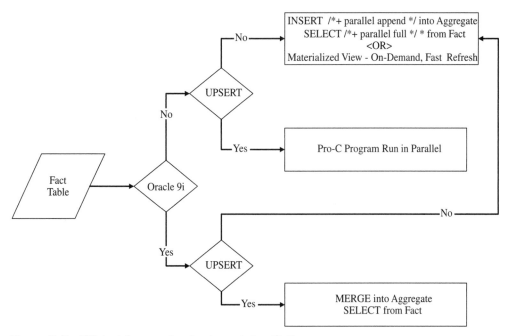

Figure 7–5 Efficient Aggregation Implementation Options

To provide context for the following descriptions of these three aggregation scenarios, refer once again to this book's simple data warehousing data model shown in Figure 7–6.

Scenario 1

If you only need inserts (i.e., not upserts), then you have two fact table implementation options with this scenario: aggregate tables or materialized views.

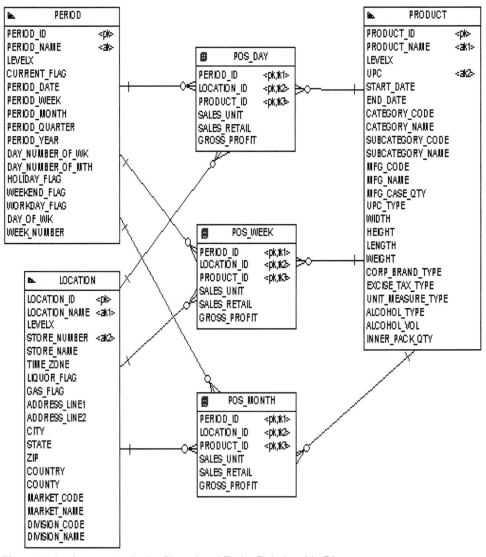

Figure 7–6 Aggregates in the Dimesional Entity Relationship Diagram

If you're using simple aggregate tables (i.e., not materialized views), then your best and most obvious choice is to merely use a simple, parallel, direct mode load insert. There is absolutely no need to write procedural logic such as Pro-C or PL/SQL code. The parallel insert with direct mode load shown below will smoke any cursor-based Pro-C or PL/SQL alternative:

```
alter session enable parallel dml;

insert /*+ parallel(aggr,10) append */
into pos_week aggr
select   /*+ parallel(fact,10) full(fact) */
  $WEEK_ID, location_id, product_id
  sum(nvl(sales_unit,0)),
  sum(nvl(sales_retail,0)),
  sum(nvl(gross_profit,0))
from pos_day fact
where period_id between $BEG_ID and $END_ID
group by $WEEK_ID, location_id, product_id;

commit;
```

How does this work? The `insert select` command expects three key pieces of information passed in as parameters: the beginning and ending period IDs for the days represented by the target week and the period ID for the target week itself. The `select` portion of the command performs group operations on the selected rows to summarize the correct aggregate data. This selection is done in parallel as indicated by the `select parallel` hint. Then, the `insert` portion of the command inserts that data in direct load mode (i.e., no logging) as indicated by the `insert append` hint. This too is done in parallel.

In the example above, note that Oracle will fork 31 processes to perform this command: a coordinator process (the controlling parent for other processes), 10 select sub-processes, 10 sort sub-processes, and 10 insert sub-processes. Don't forget, the inserts will utilize direct mode loads. That's one heck of a lot of work being done in parallel and with great efficiency, and all controlled by a few simple Oracle DML and query hints.

Of course, you'll probably have multiple target weeks that need to be aggregated. So, you could enclose the code above in a script that loops through those weeks and calls the code once per week. You could even submit those invocations in the background such that all of them could be running at once. Just make sure not to go overboard on your total parallel processing load.

Two simple rules for selecting the optimal parallel DML degree for your hardware is that the total number of parallel processes should equal:

- *No. of CPUs when CPU Bandwidth >= Disk I/O Bandwidth*
- *2– 4 * No. of CPUs When Disk I/O Bandwidth Much > CPU Bandwidth*

For example, at 7-Eleven, we had 16 CPUs and an EMC disk array with 4 GB of cache using RAID 0+1, so a total parallel process load of 32–64 concurrent processes was both sustainable and optimal (depending on the DML operations). In other words, our disk array could handle much more volume than our CPUs could generate, so we could increase our parallel degree greater than our CPU count until the disk I/O peaked.

To give you an idea of just how efficient this approach is, at 7-Eleven, we could recreate from scratch an entire 500-million-row aggregate in about 20 minutes!

Of course, Scenario 1 is also a perfect fit for materialized views. The solution would be as follows:

```
create materialized view mv_pos_week
parallel (degree 1) nologging
BUILD IMMEDIATE
REFRESH FAST
ENABLE QUERY REWRITE
as
select  /*+ parallel(pos_day,1) full(pos_day) */
  period.wk_id period_id, location_id, product_id,
  sum(nvl(sales_unit,0)),
  sum(nvl(sales_retail,0)),
  sum(nvl(gross_profit,0))
from pos_day,
     (select a.period_id wk_id, b.period_id d1_id, c.period_id
d2_id
```

```
      from period a,
           period b,
           period c
      where a.levelx='WEEK'
        and b.levelx='DAY'
        and c.levelx='DAY'
        and a.period_date     = b.period_date
        and a.period_date + 6 = c.period_date
        and exists (select 1
                      from pos_day
                         where period_id between b.period_id and
c.period_id
                    )
      ) period
where period_id between period.d1_id and period.d2_id
group by period.wk_id, location_id, product_id;
```

This code creates a fully populated aggregate implemented as a materialized view—with on-demand fast refreshes. That's all there is to it! Of course, you still need to create all the fact table bitmap indexes and statistics on the materialized view such that queries will use the star transformation explain plan. But otherwise, it's just like any other fact table.

Scenario 2

If you need upserts and you're using Oracle 8i, then your only choice is, unfortunately, to write procedural logic such as PL/SQL or Pro-C code. For many cases, Pro-C will be the superior choice in terms of raw performance.

Why Pro-C instead of just using PL/SQL? This is a fair question. PL/SQL is a great language for doing database internal programming, and that's exactly what we have here with essentially a "table to table" copy. Furthermore, SQL Plus is a lightweight command-line program that we could easily embed within UNIX shell scripts to execute PL/SQL code. So again, why not just use PL/SQL?

Remember that my goal is to show you the most optimally efficient implementation, which is Pro-C. For many shops, the answer will be to go with PL/SQL. The rationale is often that their developers are more comfortable with PL/SQL (at least more so than with

Pro-C and its associated makefiles). Plus, some UNIX vendors no longer provide a free C compiler (and Oracle currently only supports the GNU-C compiler on Linux). If that describes your shop, then by all means, stick with PL/SQL.

Prior to Oracle 9i, PL/SQL lacks one key programming construct that Pro-C provides: Dynamic SQL Method #2: prepare and execute. This programming technique can shave about 15–20% off data loading program runtimes, so in many cases, it's worth the extra costs. How does this technique work? Remember, every time Oracle processes a command, it must parse, bind, execute, and fetch. With Dynamic SQL Method #2, you can prepare a statement once outside of your loop processing and then execute it repeatedly in the loop without Oracle having to reparse or rebind it. So, your Pro-C program would look like:

```
int main(int argc, char *argv[]) {
  ...
  EXEC SQL DECLARE C1 CURSOR FOR
    select  /*+ parallel(fact,10) full(fact) */
      :WEEK_ID, location_id, product_id
      sum(nvl(sales_unit,0)),
      sum(nvl(sales_retail,0)),
      sum(nvl(gross_profit,0))
    from pos_day fact
    where period_id between :BEG_ID and :END_ID
    group by :WEEK_ID, location_id, product_id;

  strcpy(sql_command,"UPDATE pos_week \
    SET sales_unit = nvl(sales_unit,0) + \
            :h_sales_unit:i_sales_unit, \
        sales_retail = nvl(sales_retail,0) + \
            :h_sales_retail:i_sales_retail, \
        gross_profit = nvl(gross_profit,0) + \
            :h_gross_profit:i_gross_profit \
    WHERE period_id = :h_period_id:i_period_id \
      AND location_id = :h_location_id:i_location_id \
      AND product_id = :h_product_id:i_product_id;"
  EXEC SQL PREPARE update_command FROM :sql_command;

  strcpy(sql_command,"INSERT INTO pos_week VALUES \
    (:h_period_id:i_period_id, \
     :h_location_id:i_location_id, \
```

```
        :h_product_id:i_product_id, \
        :h_sales_unit:i_sales_unit,
        :h_sales_retail:i_sales_retail, \
        :h_gross_profit:i_gross_profit)");
EXEC SQL PREPARE insert_command FROM :sql_command;

EXEC SQL OPEN C1;
/* Process fact table records */
EXEC SQL FETCH C1 INTO :h_period_id:i_period_id, \
                      :h_location_id:i_location_id, \
                      :h_product_id:i_product_id, \
                      :h_sales_unit:i_sales_unit, \
                      :h_sales_retail:i_sales_retail, \
                      :h_gross_profit:i_gross_profit;
while (sqlca.sqlcode == 0) {
  ...
  /* First - try to update existing record */
  EXEC SQL EXECUTE update_command
      USING :h_period_id:i_period_id, \
            :h_location_id:i_location_id, \
            :h_product_id:i_product_id, \
            :h_sales_unit:i_sales_unit,
            :h_sales_retail:i_sales_retail, \
            :h_gross_profit:i_gross_profit;

  /* Second - if update fails because record
              not found, then insert record*/
  if (sqlca.sqlcode == 1403) {
    EXEC SQL EXECUTE insert_command
      USING :h_period_id:i_period_id, \
            :h_location_id:i_location_id, \
            :h_product_id:i_product_id, \
            :h_sales_unit:i_sales_unit,
            :h_sales_retail:i_sales_retail, \
            :h_gross_profit:i_gross_profit;
  }
  else if (sqlca.sqlcode != 0) {
    ...
  }
  ...
  EXEC SQL FETCH C1 INTO :h_period_id:i_period_id, \
                        :h_location_id:i_location_id, \
                        :h_product_id:i_product_id, \
```

```
                              :h_sales_unit:i_sales_unit,
                              :h_sales_retail:i_sales_retail, \
                              :h_gross_profit:i_gross_profit;

  }
  EXEC SQL CLOSE C1;
  ...
}
```

Of course, you'll probably have multiple target weeks that need to be aggregated. So, you could enclose the program call for the code above in a script that loops through those weeks and calls the program once per week. You should submit those invocations in the background such that some or even all of them could be running in parallel. Unlike Scenario 1, which would run both the insert and select in parallel, Scenario 2 only runs the select command in parallel—and only for the execute stage—but the fetched records are processed serially. That's why you should run this scenario with more parallel background invocations.

As before, the total parallel DML processes should equal:

- *No. of CPUs When CPU Bandwidth >= Disk I/O Bandwidth*
- *2– 4 * No. of CPUs When Disk I/O Bandwidth Much > CPU Bandwidth*

Scenario 3

If you need upserts and you're using Oracle 9i, then you'll want to use the new MERGE command. It's simply a new DML command that encapsulates an UPDATE and INSERT into a single command processed by a single call to the database. Your developers will love this new syntax, as it's exactly what they've been coding as separate, related DML commands with intelligent error handling. Now it is a single command, and a single network request sent to the database server. So, you get the best of both worlds: easier to code and runs faster, too. Here's the code to perform our day to week aggregation:

```
alter session enable parallel dml;
merge /*+ parallel(pos_week,10) append
          parallel(pos_day,10) full(pos_day) */
    into pos_week aggr
```

```
using (select   $WEEK_ID, location_id, product_id
          sum(nvl(sales_unit,0)),
          sum(nvl(sales_retail,0)),
          sum(nvl(gross_profit,0))
       from pos_day
       where period_id between $BEG_ID and $END_ID
       group by :WEEK_ID, location_id, product_id) fact
on (fact.period_id    = aggr.period_id and
    fact.location_id = aggr.location_id and
    fact.product_id   = aggr.product_id)
when matched then
    update set
       c4 = nvl(f.c4,0) + nvl(y.c4),
       C5 = nvl(f.c5,0) + nvl(y.c5),
       C6 = nvl(f.c4,0) + nvl(y.c4) +
            nvl(f.c5,0) + nvl(y.c5) - y.av
when not matched then
    insert values ();
```

An interesting thought is that you may be able to capitalize on the efficiency of the new MERGE command to eek out a few more parallel processes. With MERGE, you can consider amending your total parallel DML processes to:

- *1.5 * No. of CPUs When CPU Bandwidth >= Disk I/O Bandwidth*
- *2.5– 4 * No. of CPUs When Disk I/O Bandwidth Much > CPU Bandwidth*

One final note: You cannot implement this technique with materialized views as the refresh mechanism only supports queries (and not the MERGE command—yet).

USE MATERIALIZED VIEWS

As for aggregates, you should always implement them as materialized views, period. First, no matter what business intelligence tool your end-users select, query rewrites can be accomplished and are desirable. Second, regardless of which aggregation method you implement from the previous section, they all will work equally well against a materialized view (since it's nothing more than a locally replicated table).

There are no downsides to implementing aggregates as materialized views, therefore you should always do so. And for those of you who already have a data warehouse built, go back and create materialized views on your pre-existing aggregate tables. This way, you too can get query rewrites even though you're not using any other materialized view features.

Here are the basic implementation guidelines:

1. Create Oracle dimensions for each dimension table.
2. Enable dimension primary key constraints with NOVALIDATE (if they don't exist).
3. Enable fact primary key constraint with NOVALIDATE (using existing unique index).
4. Enable fact to dimension foreign key constraints with NOVALIDATE.
5. Create materialized view logs on dimensions.
6. Create a materialized view log on the base fact table.
7. Create materialized views with query rewrite enabled for aggregates.
8. Create star transformation bitmap indexes and statistics on materialized views.
9. Use Oracle Enterprise Manager's Summary Advisor to gauge effectiveness.

Detailed below are the above steps applied to this book's simple data warehousing data model shown in Figure 7–6:

1. Create Oracle dimensions for each dimension table:

```
CREATE DIMENSION time_dim
   LEVEL curdate     IS period.period_date
   LEVEL month       IS period.period_month
   LEVEL quarter     IS period.period_quarter
   LEVEL year        IS period.period_year
   LEVEL week_num    IS period.week_number
HIERARCHY calendar_rollup(
   curdate         CHILD OF
```

```
  month          CHILD OF
  quarter        CHILD OF
  year)
HIERARCHY weekly_rollup(
  curdate        CHILD OF
  week_num)
ATTRIBUTE curdate DETERMINES period.day_of_wk;
```

2. Enable dimension primary key constraints with NOVALIDATE (if they don't exist):

```
alter table period
    add constraint period_pk
    primary key (period_id)
    novalidate;
alter table location
    add constraint location_pk
    primary key (location_id)
    novalidate;
alter table product
    add constraint product_pk
    primary key (product_id)
    novalidate;
```

3. Enable fact primary key constraint with NOVALIDATE (using existing unique index):

```
alter table pos_day
    add constraint pos_day_pk
    primary key (PERIOD_ID, LOCATION_ID, PRODUCT_ID)
    using index pos_day_pk
    novalidate;
```

4. Enable fact to dimension foreign key constraints with NOVALIDATE:

```
alter table pos_day
    add constraint pos_day_fk1
       foreign key (period_id) references period(period_id)
    novalidate;

alter table pos_day
    add constraint pos_day_fk2
    foreign key (location_id) references location(location_id)
```

```
    novalidate;

alter table pos_day
    add constraint pos_day_fk3
    foreign key (product_id) references product(product_id)
    novalidate;
```

5. Create materialized view logs on dimensions:

```
create materialized view log on period
  WITH SEQUENCE, ROWID
(
 PERIOD_ID,
 PERIOD_NAME,
 LEVELX,
 CURRENT_FLAG,
 PERIOD_DATE,
 PERIOD_WEEK,
 PERIOD_MONTH,
 PERIOD_QUARTER,
 PERIOD_YEAR,
 DAY_NUMBER_OF_WK,
 DAY_NUMBER_OF_MTH,
 HOLIDAY_FLAG,
 WEEKEND_FLAG,
 WORKDAY_FLAG,
 DAY_OF_WK,
 WEEK_NUMBER
)
INCLUDING NEW VALUES;
```

6. Create a materialized view log on the base fact table:

```
create materialized view log on pos_day
  WITH SEQUENCE, ROWID
(
 PERIOD_ID,
 LOCATION_ID,
 PRODUCT_ID,
 SALES_UNIT,
 SALES_RETAIL,
 GROSS_PROFIT
)
INCLUDING NEW VALUES;
```

7. Create materialized views with query rewrite enabled for aggregates:

```
create materialized view mv_pos_week
parallel (degree 1) nologging
BUILD IMMEDIATE
REFRESH FAST
ENABLE QUERY REWRITE
as
select  /*+ parallel(pos_day,1) full(pos_day) */
  period.wk_id period_id, location_id, product_id,
  sum(nvl(sales_unit,0)),
  sum(nvl(sales_retail,0)),
  sum(nvl(gross_profit,0))
from pos_day,
      (select a.period_id wk_id, b.period_id d1_id, c.period_id
d2_id
      from period a,
           period b,
           period c
      where a.levelx='WEEK'
        and b.levelx='DAY'
        and c.levelx='DAY'
        and a.period_date     = b.period_date
        and a.period_date + 6 = c.period_date
        and exists (select 1
                    from pos_day
                        where period_id between b.period_id and
c.period_id
                   )
      ) period
where period_id between period.d1_id and period.d2_id
group by period.wk_id, location_id, product_id;
```

8. Create star transformation bitmap indexes and statistics on materialized views:

```
CREATE BITMAP INDEX MV_POS_WEEK_B1 ON MV_POS_WEEK (PERIOD_ID)
      PCTFREE 1
      NOLOGGING;

CREATE BITMAP INDEX MV_POS_WEEK_B2 ON MV_POS_WEEK (LOCATION_ID)
      PCTFREE 1
      NOLOGGING;
```

```
CREATE BITMAP INDEX MV_POS_WEEK_B3 ON MV_POS_WEEK (PRODUCT_ID)
      PCTFREE 1
      NOLOGGING;

analyze table mv_pos_week
   estimate statistics
   for table
   for all indexes
   for all indexed columns sample 20000 rows;
```

9. Use Oracle Enterprise Manager's Summary Advisor to gauge effectiveness (shown in Figure 7–7)

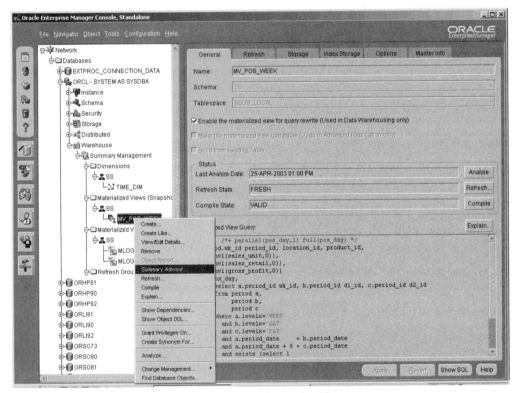

Figure 7–7   Summary Management via Oracle Enterprise Manager

CHAPTER 8

Partitioning for Manageability

Back in Chapter 3, two critical points were made: Fact tables are so large that your success will largely hinge on their implementation, and fact tables should be partitioned to improve their manageability, not for quicker end-user ad-hoc queries or faster data load times.

I find that most DBAs eagerly partition their facts since it seems intuitively obvious that anything that large should be partitioned. However, they often partition their facts for the wrong reasons, and sometimes using the wrong, or even the worst, partitioning criteria. About half do so to improve query response times. The belief is that the best queries are those done in parallel against partitioned and sub-partitioned tables. But the fact is (as explained back in Chapter 5) that obtaining the star transformation explain plan is the most critical aspect for ad-hoc queries. In fact, it is so important that it does not really matter whether the table is partitioned or not. Yes, queries will run faster against partitioned fact tables, but 98% of the query speed will be from achieving the correct star transformation explain plan. Partitioning will simply be "icing on the cake" in terms of speeding up the end-users' ad-hoc queries.

Therefore, DBAs typically partition for the wrong reasons, and possibly sub-optimally as well. For example, consider the DBA who partitions a fact along a non-time dimension as many queries reference that criteria. In this case, the DBA is actually partitioning along a candidate for aggregation in the mistaken belief that it will speed up queries. Don't confuse partitioning and aggregation; they serve very different purposes.

Other DBAs partition their facts to improve data loading batch cycles. But remember, adding rows to a table really is not dependent on the size of that table. You can add a million rows to a billion-row table just about as fast as to an empty one, especially using the APPEND hint to achieve direct mode loads. The real time savings here is that you can drop and recreate indexes on the affected partitions rather than for the entire table. This is really a divide and conquer technique for managing very long-running and costly operations. In other words, these DBAs are actually and unknowingly doing the right thing for the wrong reasons. But typically, they do get the partitioning criteria correct.

One last issue that often muddies the water regarding fact table partitioning is this: DBAs may define their partitioning schema under Oracle 8i (with its numerous limitations), and then not revisit that design when upgrading to Oracle 9i. For example, Oracle 8i does not offer list partitioning and only permits parallel operations across partitions, not within them. However, Oracle 9i offers list partitioning and permits parallel operations both across and within partitions. The point is that when either selecting an Oracle version or upgrading, you should re-evaluate the current partitioning design so as to best leverage what's now available. Otherwise, you may well end up with a partitioning scheme that is sub-optimal for your Oracle version.

A PLETHORA OF DESIGN OPTIONS

One of the first things to do before designing your fact tables is to fully understand your entire range of table and index implementation options (shown in Figure 8–1). If nothing else, this plethora of design options should very clearly explain why DBAs are necessary. Far too many developers "want to be" DBAs and don't really know all the possible options for implementing a table. These types are often shocked by Figure 8–1.

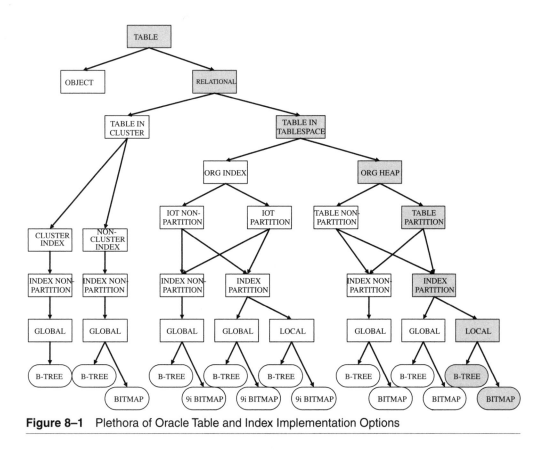

Figure 8–1 Plethora of Oracle Table and Index Implementation Options

The key point (objects shaded in gray in Figure 8–1) is to follow the right-hand side of this tree of options. Namely, facts should be simple, heap-organized tables that are partitioned. And their indexes should be locally partitioned (i.e., each table partition has a matching index partition). The fact's unique index should be a local, prefixed b-tree, while all the remaining indexes should be bitmaps. Assuming that you partition by time, the time dimension-based bitmap will most likely be a local, prefixed bitmap index, while the others will be local, non-prefixed bitmaps.

And that brings us to picking a stated design direction and then implementing it.

LOGICAL PARTITIONING DESIGN

The first thing you must decide is how you'll want to partition your fact tables. In 90% of the cases I've seen, the DBA simply chooses to implement a sliding window of data over time, with individual partitions each representing a reasonable time slice of the data over that time (as shown in Figure 8–2). We'll refer to this as simple partitioning.

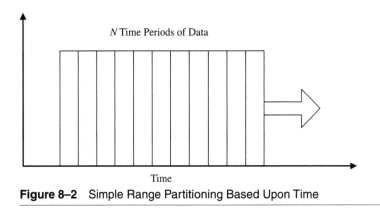

Figure 8–2   Simple Range Partitioning Based Upon Time

Note that this is not a technical design decision, but really much more of a business requirement. What I mean is that your end-users will tell you to keep *N* time periods of data online and how often to load or update it. The only technical issue is how to best support archiving data as it logically falls off the trailing edge.

If you were not partitioned by time, then you'd have to use a very slow DML command such as `DELETE FROM fact WHERE period_id < cut off value` to remove old records. Not only would that take an extremely long time, but it also could unbalance b-tree indexes and fragment tablespaces. A much better solution is to simply drop off the expired partition using the `ALTER TABLE fact DROP PARTITION x` command.

As an example of end-user input, the business requirements may mandate keeping 60 months (i.e., 5 years) of data, which is updated nightly. So if the DBA chooses to partition by month, then at most, the database will have 61 partitions, each of which must hold approximately 30 days' worth of data. If the nightly cycle loads 20 million records, then a fact partition will hold approximately 600 million rows. If, on the other hand, the DBA chooses to partition by week, then at most, the database will have 261 partitions, each of which will hold 7 days' worth of data, or about 140 million rows.

Which is better? It all depends, but in general, the more granular the partition the better. The reason is that a few hundred million rows is a reasonable figure for DDL operations such as creating an index, and smaller, more granular partitions should not exceed this size. Furthermore, the logic to handle weekly partitions is much simpler since all weeks have exactly the same number of days. Monthly partitions have a huge drawback in that the logic to handle them must handle the various months' day counts, including the often-forgotten leap years, where February has 29 versus the normal 28 days. It's much better to keep partition management logic simple and partition size small (relatively speaking, of course).

There are two other less obvious reasons why smaller partitions work better. First, for queries and DML that must access a partition, smaller partitions can lead to a higher degree of parallel operations, especially with Oracle 8i, which generally does not support parallel operations within a partition. So, having more partitions is a manual method for forcing potentially higher degrees of parallel operations. However, this situation no longer exists with Oracle 9i. Thus, I would not recommend adopting an approach that has already been addressed, especially since 9i is in its second release already.

A second and less important reason for more, smaller partitions is that they more naturally support logical aggregation options. For example, week partitions very naturally and easily summarize into weeks, months, quarters, and years. But larger partitions such as months do not. While this is not a show-stopper in terms of whether or not you should do it, I would recommend considering this within the context of all the other issues you may need to balance. In other words, it might be useful as a tie-breaker.

As I said, 90% of DBAs just do the above. However, I've seen about 10% take it a step further. They partition first by time and then sub-partition along some other criteria, either dimensionally based or specially designed for their needs. Essentially, the idea is to subdivide time partitions into additional and even smaller sub-partitions (as shown in Figure 8–3). We'll refer to this as complex partitioning

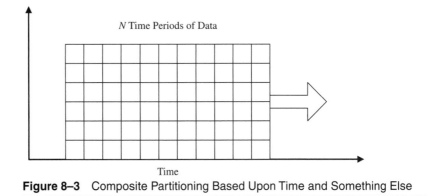

Figure 8–3 Composite Partitioning Based Upon Time and Something Else

One of the chief reasons DBAs do this is to achieve parallel joins between facts and dimensions, where the dimension is partitioned along the same criteria as the fact. Oracle refers to this as partition-wise joins, and they are very useful for parallel server environments. The problem is that very few of the DBAs I've seen implementing this feature have parallel servers. Again, they most often do it for theoretically improving query runtimes. And as before, while it may speed up queries somewhat, it's only the star transformation that really matters. This would just be another "icing on the cake" improvement.

Another reason I see DBAs doing sub-partitioning is the belief that they can achieve sub-partition elimination, and thus again speed up queries. The problem is that more often than not, this may actually make things worse. Let me explain. Oracle 8i offers range partitions that can be sub-partitioned by hashing, whereas Oracle 9i now offers range partitions that can be sub-partitioned by lists or hashing. Either way, you must fully understand the underlying nature of your data to make effective use of these features. The sub-partitioning scheme must conform to the nature of your data, or you may actually makes things much worse.

For example, I tried hashed sub-partitions with 7-Eleven's data warehouse. I partitioned by range on my period identifier, making each partition contain a week's worth of data. Then I hash-sub-partitioned on my product identifier. The idea was that similar products would hash into the same sub-partitions, thus queries on classes of products (such as beer) would only reference those sub-partitions.

Sounds good, right? But, I had overlooked the nature of my data. The product identifiers were surrogate or meaningless keys and thus evenly distributed across the entire product identifier domain. Therefore, hashing merely spread my data equally across all the sub-partitions and required an extra level of sub-partition operations to obtain the exact same data. So, my queries took twice as long. Needless to say, I went back to just range partitioning without sub-partitions.

SIMPLE PARTITIONING IN 8I

With Oracle 8i, there is only one way to implement simple partitioning: with range partitioning (as shown below):

```
CREATE TABLE POS_DAY_RNG
  PCTFREE 10
  PCTUSED 89
  PARALLEL (DEGREE 10)
  NOLOGGING
  PARTITION BY RANGE (period_id)
    (
       PARTITION p001 VALUES LESS THAN (1073),
       PARTITION p002 VALUES LESS THAN (1081),
       PARTITION p003 VALUES LESS THAN (1089),
       PARTITION p004 VALUES LESS THAN (1097),
       PARTITION p005 VALUES LESS THAN (1105),
       PARTITION p006 VALUES LESS THAN (1113),
       PARTITION p007 VALUES LESS THAN (1121),
       PARTITION p008 VALUES LESS THAN (1129),
       PARTITION p009 VALUES LESS THAN (1137),
       ...
    )
AS
 SELECT /*+ parallel(pos_day) full(pos_day) */ *
 FROM pos_day;

CREATE UNIQUE INDEX POS_DAY_RNG_PK
  ON POS_DAY_RNG (PERIOD_ID, LOCATION_ID, PRODUCT_ID)
  PCTFREE 1
  PARALLEL (DEGREE 10)
  NOLOGGING
  LOCAL;

CREATE BITMAP INDEX POS_DAY_RNG_B1
```

```
   ON POS_DAY_RNG (PERIOD_ID)
   PCTFREE 1
   PARALLEL (DEGREE 10)
   NOLOGGING
   LOCAL;

CREATE BITMAP INDEX POS_DAY_RNG_B2
   ON POS_DAY_RNG (LOCATION_ID)
   PCTFREE 1
   PARALLEL (DEGREE 10)
   NOLOGGING
   LOCAL;

CREATE BITMAP INDEX POS_DAY_RNG_B3
   ON POS_DAY_RNG (PRODUCT_ID)
   PCTFREE 1
   PARALLEL (DEGREE 10)
   NOLOGGING
   LOCAL;
```

Oracle defines range partitioning as a method that maps data to partitions based on ranges of partition key values that you establish for each partition. It is the most common type of partitioning and is often used with dates (see the *Oracle 9i Concepts* manual).

Note that the space requirements for this partitioning method are very straightforward and simple. Each partition and index partition creates one segment. Let's assume we created just four partitions, p001 through p004; we'd thus create a grand total of 20 segments (shown below):

SEGMENT_NAME	PARTITION_NAME	SEGMENT_TYPE	BYTES
POS_DAY_LST	P001	TABLE PARTITION	65,536
POS_DAY_LST	P002	TABLE PARTITION	65,536
POS_DAY_LST	P003	TABLE PARTITION	65,536
POS_DAY_LST	P004	TABLE PARTITION	65,536
POS_DAY_LST_B1	P001	INDEX PARTITION	65,536
POS_DAY_LST_B1	P002	INDEX PARTITION	65,536
POS_DAY_LST_B1	P003	INDEX PARTITION	65,536
POS_DAY_LST_B1	P004	INDEX PARTITION	65,536
POS_DAY_LST_B2	P001	INDEX PARTITION	65,536
POS_DAY_LST_B2	P002	INDEX PARTITION	65,536
POS_DAY_LST_B2	P003	INDEX PARTITION	65,536
POS_DAY_LST_B2	P004	INDEX PARTITION	65,536
POS_DAY_LST_B3	P001	INDEX PARTITION	65,536

POS_DAY_LST_B3	P002	INDEX PARTITION	65,536
POS_DAY_LST_B3	P003	INDEX PARTITION	65,536
POS_DAY_LST_B3	P004	INDEX PARTITION	65,536
POS_DAY_LST_PK	P001	INDEX PARTITION	65,536
POS_DAY_LST_PK	P002	INDEX PARTITION	65,536
POS_DAY_LST_PK	P003	INDEX PARTITION	65,536
POS_DAY_LST_PK	P004	INDEX PARTITION	65,536

```
20 rows selected.
```

SIMPLE PARTITIONING IN 9I

With Oracle 9i, there are two ways to implement simple partitioning: with range partitioning (exactly the same as shown in the prior section) or with list partitioning (as shown below):

```
CREATE TABLE POS_DAY_LST
  PCTFREE 10
  PCTUSED 89
  PARALLEL (DEGREE 10)
  NOLOGGING
  PARTITION BY LIST (period_id)
    (
      PARTITION p001 VALUES
        (1065,1066,1067,1068,1069,1070,1071,1072),
      PARTITION p002 VALUES
        (1073,1074,1075,1076,1077,1078,1079,1080),
      PARTITION p003 VALUES
        (1081,1082,1083,1084,1085,1086,1087,1088),
      PARTITION p004 VALUES
        (1089,1090,1091,1092,1093,1094,1095,1096),
      PARTITION p005 VALUES
        (1097,1098,1099,1100,1101,1102,1103,1104),
      PARTITION p006 VALUES
        (1105,1106,1107,1108,1109,1110,1111,1112),
      PARTITION p007 VALUES
        (1113,1114,1115,1116,1117,1118,1119,1120),
      PARTITION p008 VALUES
        (1121,1122,1123,1124,1125,1126,1127,1128),
      PARTITION p009 VALUES
        (1129,1130,1131,1132,1133,1134,1135,1136),
      ...
    )
AS
```

```
SELECT /*+ parallel(pos_day) full(pos_day) */ *
FROM pos_day;

CREATE UNIQUE INDEX POS_DAY_LST_PK
  ON POS_DAY_LST (PERIOD_ID, LOCATION_ID, PRODUCT_ID)
  PCTFREE 1
  PARALLEL (DEGREE 10)
  NOLOGGING
  LOCAL;

CREATE BITMAP INDEX POS_DAY_LST_B1
  ON POS_DAY_LST (PERIOD_ID)
  PCTFREE 1
  PARALLEL (DEGREE 10)
  NOLOGGING
  LOCAL;

CREATE BITMAP INDEX POS_DAY_LST_B2
  ON POS_DAY_LST (LOCATION_ID)
  PCTFREE 1
  PARALLEL (DEGREE 10)
  NOLOGGING
  LOCAL;

CREATE BITMAP INDEX POS_DAY_LST_B3
  ON POS_DAY_LST (PRODUCT_ID)
  PCTFREE 1
  PARALLEL (DEGREE 10)
  NOLOGGING
  LOCAL;
```

Oracle defines list partitioning as a method that enables you to explicitly control how rows map to partitions. You do this by specifying a list of discrete values for the partitioning key in the description of each partition. The advantage of list partitioning is that you can group and organize unordered and unrelated sets of data in a natural way (see the *Oracle 9i Concepts* manual).

Note that the space requirements for this partitioning method are also very straightforward and simple. Again, each partition and index partition create one segment. Let's assume we created just four partitions, p001 through p004; we'd thus create a grand total of 20 segments (shown below):

```
SEGMENT_NAME          PARTITION_NAME   SEGMENT_TYPE           BYTES
------------------    --------------   -----------------    --------
POS_DAY_LST           P001             TABLE PARTITION        65,536
POS_DAY_LST           P002             TABLE PARTITION        65,536
POS_DAY_LST           P003             TABLE PARTITION        65,536
POS_DAY_LST           P004             TABLE PARTITION        65,536
POS_DAY_LST_B1        P001             INDEX PARTITION        65,536
POS_DAY_LST_B1        P002             INDEX PARTITION        65,536
POS_DAY_LST_B1        P003             INDEX PARTITION        65,536
POS_DAY_LST_B1        P004             INDEX PARTITION        65,536
POS_DAY_LST_B2        P001             INDEX PARTITION        65,536
POS_DAY_LST_B2        P002             INDEX PARTITION        65,536
POS_DAY_LST_B2        P003             INDEX PARTITION        65,536
POS_DAY_LST_B2        P004             INDEX PARTITION        65,536
POS_DAY_LST_B3        P001             INDEX PARTITION        65,536
POS_DAY_LST_B3        P002             INDEX PARTITION        65,536
POS_DAY_LST_B3        P003             INDEX PARTITION        65,536
POS_DAY_LST_B3        P004             INDEX PARTITION        65,536
POS_DAY_LST_PK        P001             INDEX PARTITION        65,536
POS_DAY_LST_PK        P002             INDEX PARTITION        65,536
POS_DAY_LST_PK        P003             INDEX PARTITION        65,536
POS_DAY_LST_PK        P004             INDEX PARTITION        65,536

20 rows selected.
```

COMPLEX PARTITIONING IN 8I

With Oracle 8i, there is only one way to implement complex partition-ing: with composite range-hash partitioning (as shown below):

```
CREATE TABLE POS_DAY_RNG_HSH
  PCTFREE 10
  PCTUSED 89
  PARALLEL (DEGREE 10)
  NOLOGGING
  PARTITION BY RANGE (period_id)
  SUBPARTITION BY HASH(product_id)
  SUBPARTITION TEMPLATE
    (
      SUBPARTITION sp001,
      SUBPARTITION sp002,
      SUBPARTITION sp003,
      SUBPARTITION sp004
    )
```

```
    (
      PARTITION p001 VALUES LESS THAN (1073),
      PARTITION p002 VALUES LESS THAN (1081),
      PARTITION p003 VALUES LESS THAN (1089),
      PARTITION p004 VALUES LESS THAN (1097),
      PARTITION p005 VALUES LESS THAN (1105),
      PARTITION p006 VALUES LESS THAN (1113),
      PARTITION p007 VALUES LESS THAN (1121),
      PARTITION p008 VALUES LESS THAN (1129),
      PARTITION p009 VALUES LESS THAN (1137),
      ...
    )
AS
 SELECT /*+ parallel(pos_day) full(pos_day) */ *
 FROM pos_day;

CREATE UNIQUE INDEX POS_DAY_RNG_HSH_PK
  ON POS_DAY_RNG_HSH (PERIOD_ID, LOCATION_ID, PRODUCT_ID)
  PCTFREE 1
  PARALLEL (DEGREE 10)
  NOLOGGING
  LOCAL;

CREATE BITMAP INDEX POS_DAY_RNG_HSH_B1
  ON POS_DAY_RNG_HSH (PERIOD_ID)
  PCTFREE 1
  PARALLEL (DEGREE 10)
  NOLOGGING
  LOCAL;

CREATE BITMAP INDEX POS_DAY_RNG_HSH_B2
  ON POS_DAY_RNG_HSH (LOCATION_ID)
  PCTFREE 1
  PARALLEL (DEGREE 10)
  NOLOGGING
  LOCAL;

CREATE BITMAP INDEX POS_DAY_RNG_HSH_B3
  ON POS_DAY_RNG_HSH (PRODUCT_ID)
  PCTFREE 1
  PARALLEL (DEGREE 10)
  NOLOGGING
  LOCAL;
```

Oracle states that composite range-hash partitioning provides the improved manageability of range partitioning and the data placement, striping, and parallelism advantages of hash partitioning.

Note that the space requirements for this partitioning method are slightly (or much, depending on your viewpoint) more complicated. Each partition and index partition create one segment per sub-partition. Let's assume we created just four partitions, p001 through p004; we'd thus create a grand total of 80 segments (listed below). Thus, complex partitioning via sub-partitions requires the DBA to carefully plan initial and next extent sizes because there are so many segments.

SEGMENT_NAME	PARTITION_NAME	SEGMENT_TYPE	BYTES
POS_DAY_RNG_HSH	P001_SP001	TABLE SUBPARTITION	65,536
POS_DAY_RNG_HSH	P001_SP002	TABLE SUBPARTITION	65,536
POS_DAY_RNG_HSH	P001_SP003	TABLE SUBPARTITION	65,536
POS_DAY_RNG_HSH	P001_SP004	TABLE SUBPARTITION	65,536
POS_DAY_RNG_HSH	P002_SP001	TABLE SUBPARTITION	65,536
POS_DAY_RNG_HSH	P002_SP002	TABLE SUBPARTITION	65,536
POS_DAY_RNG_HSH	P002_SP003	TABLE SUBPARTITION	65,536
POS_DAY_RNG_HSH	P002_SP004	TABLE SUBPARTITION	65,536
POS_DAY_RNG_HSH	P003_SP001	TABLE SUBPARTITION	65,536
POS_DAY_RNG_HSH	P003_SP002	TABLE SUBPARTITION	65,536
POS_DAY_RNG_HSH	P003_SP003	TABLE SUBPARTITION	65,536
POS_DAY_RNG_HSH	P003_SP004	TABLE SUBPARTITION	65,536
POS_DAY_RNG_HSH	P004_SP001	TABLE SUBPARTITION	65,536
POS_DAY_RNG_HSH	P004_SP002	TABLE SUBPARTITION	65,536
POS_DAY_RNG_HSH	P004_SP003	TABLE SUBPARTITION	65,536
POS_DAY_RNG_HSH	P004_SP004	TABLE SUBPARTITION	65,536
POS_DAY_RNG_HSH_B1	P001_SP001	INDEX SUBPARTITION	65,536
POS_DAY_RNG_HSH_B1	P001_SP002	INDEX SUBPARTITION	65,536
POS_DAY_RNG_HSH_B1	P001_SP003	INDEX SUBPARTITION	65,536
POS_DAY_RNG_HSH_B1	P001_SP004	INDEX SUBPARTITION	65,536
POS_DAY_RNG_HSH_B1	P002_SP001	INDEX SUBPARTITION	65,536
POS_DAY_RNG_HSH_B1	P002_SP002	INDEX SUBPARTITION	65,536
POS_DAY_RNG_HSH_B1	P002_SP003	INDEX SUBPARTITION	65,536
POS_DAY_RNG_HSH_B1	P002_SP004	INDEX SUBPARTITION	65,536
POS_DAY_RNG_HSH_B1	P003_SP001	INDEX SUBPARTITION	65,536
POS_DAY_RNG_HSH_B1	P003_SP002	INDEX SUBPARTITION	65,536
POS_DAY_RNG_HSH_B1	P003_SP003	INDEX SUBPARTITION	65,536
POS_DAY_RNG_HSH_B1	P003_SP004	INDEX SUBPARTITION	65,536
POS_DAY_RNG_HSH_B1	P004_SP001	INDEX SUBPARTITION	65,536
POS_DAY_RNG_HSH_B1	P004_SP002	INDEX SUBPARTITION	65,536
POS_DAY_RNG_HSH_B1	P004_SP003	INDEX SUBPARTITION	65,536
POS_DAY_RNG_HSH_B1	P004_SP004	INDEX SUBPARTITION	65,536
POS_DAY_RNG_HSH_B2	P001_SP001	INDEX SUBPARTITION	65,536
POS_DAY_RNG_HSH_B2	P001_SP002	INDEX SUBPARTITION	65,536
POS_DAY_RNG_HSH_B2	P001_SP003	INDEX SUBPARTITION	65,536
POS_DAY_RNG_HSH_B2	P001_SP004	INDEX SUBPARTITION	65,536

POS_DAY_RNG_HSH_B2	P002_SP001	INDEX SUBPARTITION	65,536
POS_DAY_RNG_HSH_B2	P002_SP002	INDEX SUBPARTITION	65,536
POS_DAY_RNG_HSH_B2	P002_SP003	INDEX SUBPARTITION	65,536
POS_DAY_RNG_HSH_B2	P002_SP004	INDEX SUBPARTITION	65,536
POS_DAY_RNG_HSH_B2	P003_SP001	INDEX SUBPARTITION	65,536
POS_DAY_RNG_HSH_B2	P003_SP002	INDEX SUBPARTITION	65,536
POS_DAY_RNG_HSH_B2	P003_SP003	INDEX SUBPARTITION	65,536
POS_DAY_RNG_HSH_B2	P003_SP004	INDEX SUBPARTITION	65,536
POS_DAY_RNG_HSH_B2	P004_SP001	INDEX SUBPARTITION	65,536
POS_DAY_RNG_HSH_B2	P004_SP002	INDEX SUBPARTITION	65,536
POS_DAY_RNG_HSH_B2	P004_SP003	INDEX SUBPARTITION	65,536
POS_DAY_RNG_HSH_B2	P004_SP004	INDEX SUBPARTITION	65,536
POS_DAY_RNG_HSH_B3	P001_SP001	INDEX SUBPARTITION	65,536
POS_DAY_RNG_HSH_B3	P001_SP002	INDEX SUBPARTITION	65,536
POS_DAY_RNG_HSH_B3	P001_SP003	INDEX SUBPARTITION	65,536
POS_DAY_RNG_HSH_B3	P001_SP004	INDEX SUBPARTITION	65,536
POS_DAY_RNG_HSH_B3	P002_SP001	INDEX SUBPARTITION	65,536
POS_DAY_RNG_HSH_B3	P002_SP002	INDEX SUBPARTITION	65,536
POS_DAY_RNG_HSH_B3	P002_SP003	INDEX SUBPARTITION	65,536
POS_DAY_RNG_HSH_B3	P002_SP004	INDEX SUBPARTITION	65,536
POS_DAY_RNG_HSH_B3	P003_SP001	INDEX SUBPARTITION	65,536
POS_DAY_RNG_HSH_B3	P003_SP002	INDEX SUBPARTITION	65,536
POS_DAY_RNG_HSH_B3	P003_SP003	INDEX SUBPARTITION	65,536
POS_DAY_RNG_HSH_B3	P003_SP004	INDEX SUBPARTITION	65,536
POS_DAY_RNG_HSH_B3	P004_SP001	INDEX SUBPARTITION	65,536
POS_DAY_RNG_HSH_B3	P004_SP002	INDEX SUBPARTITION	65,536
POS_DAY_RNG_HSH_B3	P004_SP003	INDEX SUBPARTITION	65,536
POS_DAY_RNG_HSH_B3	P004_SP004	INDEX SUBPARTITION	65,536
POS_DAY_RNG_HSH_PK	P001_SP001	INDEX SUBPARTITION	65,536
POS_DAY_RNG_HSH_PK	P001_SP002	INDEX SUBPARTITION	65,536
POS_DAY_RNG_HSH_PK	P001_SP003	INDEX SUBPARTITION	65,536
POS_DAY_RNG_HSH_PK	P001_SP004	INDEX SUBPARTITION	65,536
POS_DAY_RNG_HSH_PK	P002_SP001	INDEX SUBPARTITION	65,536
POS_DAY_RNG_HSH_PK	P002_SP002	INDEX SUBPARTITION	65,536
POS_DAY_RNG_HSH_PK	P002_SP003	INDEX SUBPARTITION	65,536
POS_DAY_RNG_HSH_PK	P002_SP004	INDEX SUBPARTITION	65,536
POS_DAY_RNG_HSH_PK	P003_SP001	INDEX SUBPARTITION	65,536
POS_DAY_RNG_HSH_PK	P003_SP002	INDEX SUBPARTITION	65,536
POS_DAY_RNG_HSH_PK	P003_SP003	INDEX SUBPARTITION	65,536
POS_DAY_RNG_HSH_PK	P003_SP004	INDEX SUBPARTITION	65,536
POS_DAY_RNG_HSH_PK	P004_SP001	INDEX SUBPARTITION	65,536
POS_DAY_RNG_HSH_PK	P004_SP002	INDEX SUBPARTITION	65,536
POS_DAY_RNG_HSH_PK	P004_SP003	INDEX SUBPARTITION	65,536
POS_DAY_RNG_HSH_PK	P004_SP004	INDEX SUBPARTITION	65,536

80 rows selected.

Finally, some people try to implement complex partitioning under Oracle 8i utilizing multi-column range partitioning. But this really is nothing more than an overcomplicated, manual workaround to approximate complex partitioning. Yes, it's quite doable. But, you as the DBA must decide if it's really worthwhile.

COMPLEX PARTITIONING IN 9I

With Oracle 9i, there are now two ways to implement complex partitioning: with composite range-hash partitioning (exactly the same as shown in the previous section) and composite range-list partitioning (as shown below). Note that we had to add the TIME–ZONE column (denoted in bold) to the primary key to sub-partition by it. Oracle requires the sub-partition criteria to be part of the primary key or unique index for the table.

```
CREATE TABLE POS_DAY_RNG_LST
  PCTFREE 10
  PCTUSED 89
  PARALLEL (DEGREE 10)
  NOLOGGING
  PARTITION BY RANGE (period_id)
  SUBPARTITION BY LIST(time_zone)
  SUBPARTITION TEMPLATE
    (
      SUBPARTITION east      VALUES ('EST'),
      SUBPARTITION central   VALUES ('CST'),
      SUBPARTITION mountain  VALUES ('MST'),
      SUBPARTITION west      VALUES ('PST')
    )
    (
      PARTITION p001 VALUES LESS THAN (1073),
      PARTITION p002 VALUES LESS THAN (1081),
      PARTITION p003 VALUES LESS THAN (1089),
      PARTITION p004 VALUES LESS THAN (1097),
      PARTITION p005 VALUES LESS THAN (1105),
      PARTITION p006 VALUES LESS THAN (1113),
      PARTITION p007 VALUES LESS THAN (1121),
      PARTITION p008 VALUES LESS THAN (1129),
      PARTITION p009 VALUES LESS THAN (1137),
      ...
    )
```

```
AS
 SELECT /*+ parallel(pos_day) full(pos_day) */ *
 FROM pos_day;

CREATE UNIQUE INDEX POS_DAY_RNG_LST_PK
  ON POS_DAY_RNG_LST (PERIOD_ID, LOCATION_ID,
                      PRODUCT_ID, TIME_ZONE)
  PCTFREE 1
  PARALLEL (DEGREE 10)
  NOLOGGING
  LOCAL;

CREATE BITMAP INDEX POS_DAY_RNG_LST_B1
  ON POS_DAY_RNG_LST (PERIOD_ID)
  PCTFREE 1
  PARALLEL (DEGREE 10)
  NOLOGGING
  LOCAL;

CREATE BITMAP INDEX POS_DAY_RNG_LST_B2
  ON POS_DAY_RNG_LST (LOCATION_ID)
  PCTFREE 1
  PARALLEL (DEGREE 10)
  NOLOGGING
  LOCAL;

CREATE BITMAP INDEX POS_DAY_RNG_LST_B3
  ON POS_DAY_RNG_LST (PRODUCT_ID)
  PCTFREE 1
  PARALLEL (DEGREE 10)
  NOLOGGING
  LOCAL;
```

Oracle states that composite range-list partitioning provides the manageability of range partitioning and the explicit control of list partitioning for sub-partitions.

Note that the space requirements for this partitioning method are slightly (or much, depending on your viewpoint) more complicated. Each partition and index partition create one segment per sub-partition. Let's assume we created just four partitions, p001 through p004; we'd thus create a grand total of 80 segments (listed below). Thus, complex partitioning via sub-partitions requires the DBA to carefully plan initial and next extent sizes because there are so many segments.

SEGMENT_NAME	PARTITION_NAME	SEGMENT_TYPE	BYTES
POS_DAY_RNG_LST	P001_CENTRAL	TABLE SUBPARTITION	65,536
POS_DAY_RNG_LST	P001_EAST	TABLE SUBPARTITION	65,536
POS_DAY_RNG_LST	P001_MOUNTAIN	TABLE SUBPARTITION	65,536
POS_DAY_RNG_LST	P001_WEST	TABLE SUBPARTITION	65,536
POS_DAY_RNG_LST	P002_CENTRAL	TABLE SUBPARTITION	65,536
POS_DAY_RNG_LST	P002_EAST	TABLE SUBPARTITION	65,536
POS_DAY_RNG_LST	P002_MOUNTAIN	TABLE SUBPARTITION	65,536
POS_DAY_RNG_LST	P002_WEST	TABLE SUBPARTITION	65,536
POS_DAY_RNG_LST	P003_CENTRAL	TABLE SUBPARTITION	65,536
POS_DAY_RNG_LST	P003_EAST	TABLE SUBPARTITION	65,536
POS_DAY_RNG_LST	P003_MOUNTAIN	TABLE SUBPARTITION	65,536
POS_DAY_RNG_LST	P003_WEST	TABLE SUBPARTITION	65,536
POS_DAY_RNG_LST	P004_CENTRAL	TABLE SUBPARTITION	65,536
POS_DAY_RNG_LST	P004_EAST	TABLE SUBPARTITION	65,536
POS_DAY_RNG_LST	P004_MOUNTAIN	TABLE SUBPARTITION	65,536
POS_DAY_RNG_LST	P004_WEST	TABLE SUBPARTITION	65,536
POS_DAY_RNG_LST_B1	P001_CENTRAL	INDEX SUBPARTITION	65,536
POS_DAY_RNG_LST_B1	P001_EAST	INDEX SUBPARTITION	65,536
POS_DAY_RNG_LST_B1	P001_MOUNTAIN	INDEX SUBPARTITION	65,536
POS_DAY_RNG_LST_B1	P001_WEST	INDEX SUBPARTITION	65,536
POS_DAY_RNG_LST_B1	P002_CENTRAL	INDEX SUBPARTITION	65,536
POS_DAY_RNG_LST_B1	P002_EAST	INDEX SUBPARTITION	65,536
POS_DAY_RNG_LST_B1	P002_MOUNTAIN	INDEX SUBPARTITION	65,536
POS_DAY_RNG_LST_B1	P002_WEST	INDEX SUBPARTITION	65,536
POS_DAY_RNG_LST_B1	P003_CENTRAL	INDEX SUBPARTITION	65,536
POS_DAY_RNG_LST_B1	P003_EAST	INDEX SUBPARTITION	65,536
POS_DAY_RNG_LST_B1	P003_MOUNTAIN	INDEX SUBPARTITION	65,536
POS_DAY_RNG_LST_B1	P003_WEST	INDEX SUBPARTITION	65,536
POS_DAY_RNG_LST_B1	P004_CENTRAL	INDEX SUBPARTITION	65,536
POS_DAY_RNG_LST_B1	P004_EAST	INDEX SUBPARTITION	65,536
POS_DAY_RNG_LST_B1	P004_MOUNTAIN	INDEX SUBPARTITION	65,536
POS_DAY_RNG_LST_B1	P004_WEST	INDEX SUBPARTITION	65,536
POS_DAY_RNG_LST_B2	P001_CENTRAL	INDEX SUBPARTITION	65,536
POS_DAY_RNG_LST_B2	P001_EAST	INDEX SUBPARTITION	65,536
POS_DAY_RNG_LST_B2	P001_MOUNTAIN	INDEX SUBPARTITION	65,536
POS_DAY_RNG_LST_B2	P001_WEST	INDEX SUBPARTITION	65,536
POS_DAY_RNG_LST_B2	P002_CENTRAL	INDEX SUBPARTITION	65,536
POS_DAY_RNG_LST_B2	P002_EAST	INDEX SUBPARTITION	65,536
POS_DAY_RNG_LST_B2	P002_MOUNTAIN	INDEX SUBPARTITION	65,536
POS_DAY_RNG_LST_B2	P002_WEST	INDEX SUBPARTITION	65,536
POS_DAY_RNG_LST_B2	P003_CENTRAL	INDEX SUBPARTITION	65,536
POS_DAY_RNG_LST_B2	P003_EAST	INDEX SUBPARTITION	65,536
POS_DAY_RNG_LST_B2	P003_MOUNTAIN	INDEX SUBPARTITION	65,536
POS_DAY_RNG_LST_B2	P003_WEST	INDEX SUBPARTITION	65,536
POS_DAY_RNG_LST_B2	P004_CENTRAL	INDEX SUBPARTITION	65,536

```
POS_DAY_RNG_LST_B2    P004_EAST        INDEX SUBPARTITION    65,536
POS_DAY_RNG_LST_B2    P004_MOUNTAIN    INDEX SUBPARTITION    65,536
POS_DAY_RNG_LST_B2    P004_WEST        INDEX SUBPARTITION    65,536
POS_DAY_RNG_LST_B3    P001_CENTRAL     INDEX SUBPARTITION    65,536
POS_DAY_RNG_LST_B3    P001_EAST        INDEX SUBPARTITION    65,536
POS_DAY_RNG_LST_B3    P001_MOUNTAIN    INDEX SUBPARTITION    65,536
POS_DAY_RNG_LST_B3    P001_WEST        INDEX SUBPARTITION    65,536
POS_DAY_RNG_LST_B3    P002_CENTRAL     INDEX SUBPARTITION    65,536
POS_DAY_RNG_LST_B3    P002_EAST        INDEX SUBPARTITION    65,536
POS_DAY_RNG_LST_B3    P002_MOUNTAIN    INDEX SUBPARTITION    65,536
POS_DAY_RNG_LST_B3    P002_WEST        INDEX SUBPARTITION    65,536
POS_DAY_RNG_LST_B3    P003_CENTRAL     INDEX SUBPARTITION    65,536
POS_DAY_RNG_LST_B3    P003_EAST        INDEX SUBPARTITION    65,536
POS_DAY_RNG_LST_B3    P003_MOUNTAIN    INDEX SUBPARTITION    65,536
POS_DAY_RNG_LST_B3    P003_WEST        INDEX SUBPARTITION    65,536
POS_DAY_RNG_LST_B3    P004_CENTRAL     INDEX SUBPARTITION    65,536
POS_DAY_RNG_LST_B3    P004_EAST        INDEX SUBPARTITION    65,536
POS_DAY_RNG_LST_B3    P004_MOUNTAIN    INDEX SUBPARTITION    65,536
POS_DAY_RNG_LST_B3    P004_WEST        INDEX SUBPARTITION    65,536
POS_DAY_RNG_LST_PK    P001_CENTRAL     INDEX SUBPARTITION    65,536
POS_DAY_RNG_LST_PK    P001_EAST        INDEX SUBPARTITION    65,536
POS_DAY_RNG_LST_PK    P001_MOUNTAIN    INDEX SUBPARTITION    65,536
POS_DAY_RNG_LST_PK    P001_WEST        INDEX SUBPARTITION    65,536
POS_DAY_RNG_LST_PK    P002_CENTRAL     INDEX SUBPARTITION    65,536
POS_DAY_RNG_LST_PK    P002_EAST        INDEX SUBPARTITION    65,536
POS_DAY_RNG_LST_PK    P002_MOUNTAIN    INDEX SUBPARTITION    65,536
POS_DAY_RNG_LST_PK    P002_WEST        INDEX SUBPARTITION    65,536
POS_DAY_RNG_LST_PK    P003_CENTRAL     INDEX SUBPARTITION    65,536
POS_DAY_RNG_LST_PK    P003_EAST        INDEX SUBPARTITION    65,536
POS_DAY_RNG_LST_PK    P003_MOUNTAIN    INDEX SUBPARTITION    65,536
POS_DAY_RNG_LST_PK    P003_WEST        INDEX SUBPARTITION    65,536
POS_DAY_RNG_LST_PK    P004_CENTRAL     INDEX SUBPARTITION    65,536
POS_DAY_RNG_LST_PK    P004_EAST        INDEX SUBPARTITION    65,536
POS_DAY_RNG_LST_PK    P004_MOUNTAIN    INDEX SUBPARTITION    65,536
POS_DAY_RNG_LST_PK    P004_WEST        INDEX SUBPARTITION    65,536

80 rows selected.
```

PARTITION OPTION BENCHMARKS

The natural question is which of these many techniques is best? Well, that all depends. You must weigh the options with regard to the nature of your data. What works best in one case may not work at all in another. That said, here's what I found on the 7-Eleven data warehouse (shown in Table 8–1).

TABLE 8–1 Performance Charcteristics for Various Table Implementation Options

Fact Implementation	Timing
Non-Partitioned Table	9,293
Range Partitioned Table	4,747
Multi-Column Range Partitioned Table	4,987
Range-Hash Partitioned Table	6,319
Range-List Partitioned Table	4,820
Non-Partitioned IOT[1]	12,508
Range Partitioned IOT	14,902

1   IOT stands for index organized table. This is a table in Oracle where both the table and its index are created and stored together as a single data structure. This can provide quicker access for tables that are fully indexed (i.e. tables where the index contains a majority or large percentage of the available columns).

From these results, we see that simple partitioning gave the best results. But, let me reiterate that these results are specific to a particular data warehouse's data and the nature of the end-users' queries. You should perform similar benchmarks against your data to be absolutely sure. Remember that what often looks good on paper may well under-perform in reality. So don't go into this with any preconceived favorites or other prejudices. Let the chips fall where they will, and implement the choice that works best for your data.

When in doubt, or if you don't have the time to benchmark, just go with simple range-based partitioning along a time dimension. In most cases, range partitioning will be a safe and near optimal choice.

Operational Issues and More

After the base database objects have been created and the initial data has been loaded, you have a candidate production data warehouse. You might begin with just a few facts and some simple aggregates, and you might have just a few hundred million rows to start, but the general concepts of how to successfully deploy and manage that data warehouse will remain exactly the same as you scale from these very humble beginnings into a full-fledged, multi-terabyte behemoth. Always bear in mind just how big you think the data warehouse will be 12 months into the future when making any operational support decisions. If you don't, then you will most definitely want to keep your resume up-to-date for when you run into the proverbial brick wall of problems as you scale above and beyond a terabyte.

The first and key thing to remember is that a data warehouse is not your traditional OLTP database. The deployment and management of the data warehouse must be treated very differently. You will generally find that much, if not most or all, of your traditional DBA bag of tricks will not be advisable or even feasible. You must very quickly learn to think well outside the box and openly embrace radically new and often unorthodox techniques, including those clearly outside the traditional Oracle DBA toolset. You also need to realize that good advice and techniques for data warehousing may make little or no sense in the OLTP world. So do not too quickly judge an idea as poor if it makes no sense. For example, OLTP DBAs would never fully index tables, but data warehouse DBAs must. The more you can let go, the more likely you are to succeed. It reminds me of the original *Star Trek* episode where Captain Kirk and crew are in the Old West and must relive the gunfight at the O.K. Corral. To survive the gunfight, they must fully disbelieve everything their senses tell them is real—anything less and they're dead. This is good advice for the aspiring data warehousing DBA.

In this final chapter, I'll present some thoughts to help you think outside the box. But I cannot fully detail any of these issues since much will depend on your customer's needs, database size, database version, operating system, hardware, and many other issues. My goal is hopefully to expand your horizons regarding the possibilities and inspire you to think well beyond the obvious or traditional solutions.

BACKUP AND RECOVERY

This is probably the least understood and often most heatedly debated DBA topic in data warehousing. Without intentionally bashing other books regarding Oracle data warehousing, let me say, that in general, the advice is short-sighted, covering only Oracle methods for backup and recovery. I genuinely mean no disrespect to these other authors, but I've never used and never advise DBAs to use Oracle tools for backup and recovery when dealing with databases this big. There are better methods out there. To simply ask whether it's hot or cold backups and then use Oracle's RMAN to do it is a disservice to your customers. You may have other options that are far superior—if you just look.

Ask yourself what your backup and recovery needs really are. Remember that this is a data warehouse, which is really nothing more than a glorified reporting system. Is point-in-time recovery really a necessity? What time limits do you have to perform backups? What time limits do you have to perform recoveries? And finally, what budget do you have to accomplish these tasks? These are the real and only questions of importance.

Far too often, DBAs think only in Oracle terms. So the questions become more Oracle-centric. Will the database be run in ARCHIVELOG mode? How many and how big must the online redo logs be? Will the database be backed up hot or cold? And will the backups be complete or incremental? Finally, how many tapes will all this take? These are the same questions that are asked in the traditional OLTP database world. But that does not make them the right questions.

If you'll forgive an absurd analogy, it's like planning a family vacation by saying that we'll drive the family sedan from New York to Los Angeles, take the scenic route, drive no more than 500 miles per day, and stay at Holiday Inns along the route. That may be a fine plan, but the first question should be: Do we have sufficient time to drive there and back? The second question should be: Can we fly for about the same money? If so, then the family sedan is neither necessary nor desirable. The key point is that too many DBAs blindly choose the family sedan (i.e., Oracle backup and recovery) when clearly better alternatives exist. You must be very creative and think outside the box.

So what does this mean? If you're using a journalized file system, such as one from Veritas, then you may be able to do hot versus cold and complete versus incremental backup and recovery at the file system level. In other words, you can use one technique for both your database and non-database files. This offers simplicity due to standardization. And in some cases, it may be superior technically as well. For example, Oracle 8.0's RMAN is not very efficient with regard to time (and I'm not convinced that 8i or 9i is any better). Yes, it saves tape space, but it scans entire data files for changes, which takes a long time. A journalized file system maintains log files of the changes, so it saves both space and time. I've used this technique without hitch. It just takes DBAs a while to digest and accept that they can do hot and incremental backups outside the database.

Another excellent option exists if you have the budget: hardware backups. How would you like to perform an online full backup of a multi-terabyte data warehouse in less than a minute? With today's RAID disk arrays, that option sometimes exists. The disk array can split a mirror off for doing the backup so the database remains open. It only takes a moment to separate the mirror. Then after the backup, the mirror is reconnected and also resynchronized for the changes that occurred during the backup. Of course, you may want your RAID 1 or 0+1 to contain two mirrors so that you always maintain data redundancy, even during a backup. Yes, this costs more money for more disks. But, disk space is very cheap and your customer may approve this. For example, I've used EMC's Time Finder for just this purpose. Moreover, I've used it for 24x7 data warehouses to load the data without interrupting production. In both cases, the hardware/ software solution was so simple and straightforward that I could concentrate on the business requirements at hand rather than the Oracle implementation. So, the real-world cost was actually much cheaper than architecting something and then supporting it.

Of course, there may still be those occasions where you cannot use either journalized file systems or hardware to solve your backup and recovery issues. Then, RMAN may be your obvious and only solution. Before devising your data warehouse backup and recovery strategy, consider these facts: First, a data warehouse loads massive amounts of data at regular intervals, say nightly. During other times and the majority of the total time, it's essentially a read-only reporting database. Second, many data loading operations and aggregations will be performed in parallel and using direct mode loads (i.e., no logging). Moreover, most index rebuilds will also be done using the NOLOGGING option. Thus, running the database in ARCHIVELOG mode may actually accomplish much less than you expect in terms of actual recoverability. And third, you can keep and reapply batch loading cycle data for re-execution as simply as you can keep redo log files.

Please don't question my intentions here. I'm not pushing for any preferred solution. I'm just making sure you fully consider the data warehousing environment before making your backup and recovery design selections. If you end up running a data warehouse in ARCHIVELOG mode, please make sure to size your log files appropriately, with lots of disk space available for short-term secondary storage. It's not uncommon for a single nightly batch cycle to generate GB of redo logs. If you don't plan for this, then you can add yet another reason for being getting paged at night—redo log devices filling up—and DBAs already have far too many reasons for being paged. Why add another?

SPACE MANAGEMENT

The two most common reasons data warehousing DBAs get paged at night is either that ETL jobs miss their "must start by" or "must complete by" time due to data volumes and job interdependencies, or ETL jobs cause Oracle errors in the range of ORA-1650 to ORA-1654 ("Unable to extend extent" for rollback segments, undo segments, temp segments, tables and indexes). There's not much that can be done about the first issue, but any competent DBA should definitely be in charge of his or her own destiny regarding the second issue. Proper space management and planning are both prudent and advisable.

For example, the screen snapshot in Figure 9–1 shows an example of a spreadsheet depicting a database's actual and projected growth over nearly a year and a half.

The upper line shows the amount of total disk space available and the lower line shows how the space is being consumed. The idea is that the DBA must know well in advance when the space will run out. While just adding more disks to an existing array may only take a few weeks to a month from order to install, getting a bigger or second disk array may take six months or longer. So, the DBA must truly be psychic regarding when space will run out. Otherwise, you can run out of space and suffer for months. Again, this is another situation where you'd better keep your resume up-to-date if you're not on top of things.

Another common and critical space management mistake I see data warehousing DBAs make is to try and keep their logical volume, tablespace, and data file management overly simple. Often I'll be brought into a troubled shop where the performance stinks and the on-call support is overwhelming (i.e., paged almost nightly). When I look into their space management, I generally find just a few logical volume groups, a few tablespaces, and lots of data files, something like what is shown in Figure 9–2.

So what's the problem here? Well, half of Tablespace #1's data files come from Volume Group #1 and half from Volume Group #2. The same is true for Tablespace #2. So let's assume that we have two fact tables: A and B. If Table A is in Tablespace #1 and Table B is in Tablespace #2, the DBA is assuming very little physical disk contention. But look at the figure again: Half of each volume group's physical volumes come from Disks 3 and 4. So, in fact, you have 50% disk contention for each object across these tablespaces. Therefore, the DBA has hot devices, even though he or she has striped across all the disks.

Date	# Active Users	IA Temp Megs	# Stores	POS Rows	POS Megs	Order Months	Order Rows	Order Megs	Prod Other Megs	Prod Total Megs	Dev DB Megs	Test DB Megs	Cust Megs	DSS Total Megs	EMC Available Megs
1-Sep-98	250	7,153	250	82,500,000	5,926	21	793,800,000	93,174	144,000	243,100	44,000	44,000	30,000	368,252	651,000
1-Oct-98	250	7,153	400	127,500,000	9,158	22	831,600,000	97,611	170,000	276,769	44,000	44,000	40,000	411,922	1,440,000
1-Nov-98	250	7,153	500	183,750,000	13,198	23	869,400,000	102,048	170,000	285,246	44,000	44,000	40,000	420,399	1,440,000
1-Dec-98	250	7,153	600	251,250,000	18,047	24	907,200,000	106,485	170,000	294,531	44,000	44,000	40,000	429,684	1,440,000
1-Jan-99	250	7,153	900	352,500,000	25,319	25	945,000,000	110,922	170,000	306,241	44,000	44,000	40,000	441,393	1,440,000
1-Feb-99	250	7,153	1200	487,500,000	35,016	26	982,800,000	115,358	300,000	450,374	44,000	44,000	50,000	595,527	1,440,000
1-Mar-99	250	7,153	1600	667,500,000	47,945	27	1,020,600,000	119,795	300,000	467,740	44,000	44,000	50,000	612,893	1,440,000
1-Apr-99	250	7,153	2000	892,500,000	64,106	28	1,058,400,000	124,232	300,000	488,339	44,000	44,000	50,000	633,491	1,440,000
1-May-99	250	7,153	2600	1,185,000,000	85,116	29	1,096,200,000	128,669	300,000	513,785	44,000	44,000	50,000	658,938	1,440,000
1-Jun-99	500	14,305	3000	1,522,500,000	109,358	30	1,134,000,000	133,106	300,000	542,464	44,000	44,000	50,000	694,769	1,440,000
1-Jul-99	500	14,305	3400	1,905,000,000	136,832	31	1,171,800,000	137,543	450,000	724,375	44,000	44,000	50,000	876,680	1,440,000
1-Aug-99	500	14,305	3800	2,332,500,000	167,539	32	1,209,600,000	141,980	450,000	759,518	44,000	44,000	70,000	931,823	1,440,000
1-Sep-99	500	14,305	4200	2,805,000,000	201,477	33	1,247,400,000	146,416	450,000	797,894	44,000	44,000	70,000	970,199	1,440,000
1-Oct-99	500	14,305	4600	3,322,500,000	238,648	34	1,285,200,000	150,853	450,000	839,501	44,000	44,000	70,000	1,011,807	1,440,000
1-Nov-99	500	14,305	5000	3,885,000,000	279,051	35	1,323,000,000	155,290	450,000	884,341	44,000	44,000	70,000	1,056,647	1,440,000
1-Dec-99	500	14,305	5400	4,492,500,000	322,687	36	1,360,800,000	159,727	450,000	932,414	44,000	44,000	70,000	1,104,719	1,440,000

Figure 9–1 Screenshot Showing Data Warehouse Growth Over Time

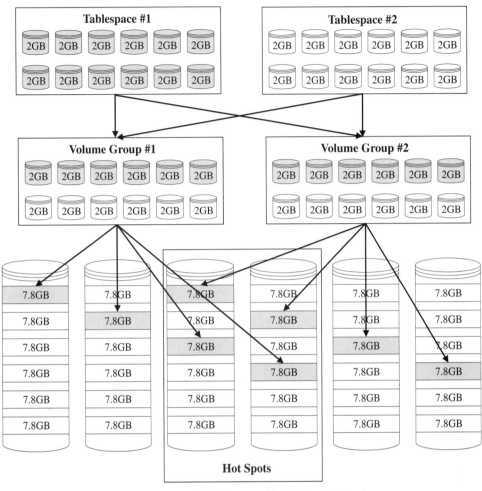

Figure 9–2 Logical Volume Manager Disk Layout with Hidden Hot Spot

The solution is to create lots of volume groups. That way, you can manually place objects into volume groups such that the overlap at the physical disk level is kept to a minimum. For example, a relatively small data warehouse (i.e., one with just a few terabytes) might have several hundred volume groups. Yes, it's going to be a small battle to convince the system administrators to create so many volume groups, but the results justify it. I've actually seen data warehouses that were near total performance failures completely turned around by simply changing the underlying volume management strategy alone.

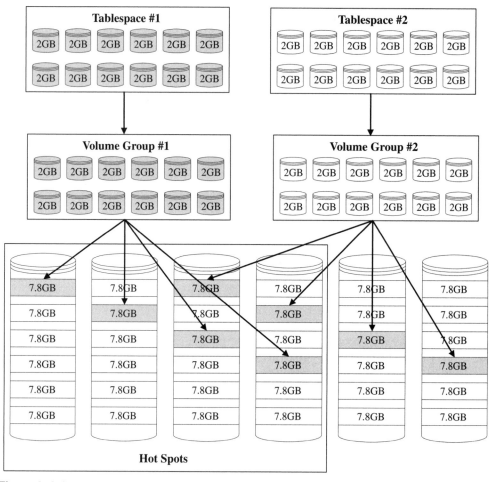

Figure 9–3 Logical Volume Manager Disk Layout with Obvious Hot Spots

One final and critical space management mistake I sometimes see data warehousing DBAs make is so obvious that I hate to bring it up: Database objects are not striped across the available volume groups. Yes, believe it or not, I've been brought into more than one situation where performance is horrible and this is the case. The culprit is a layout something like what is shown in Figure 9–3.So what's the problem here? Well, it's twofold. First, you have 50% disk contention for each object across these tablespaces (as before). Second and more importantly, you have 67% disk contention for each object in Tablespace #1. Of course, this little six physical disk scenario paints an overly negative picture. The real disk contention would be more like 12.5–25% since most LVMs permit/advise striping across from 4–8 physical disks. In real-world terms, imagine a data warehouse with, say, 256 disks and a logical volume striped across just 8 of those disks. If the DBA placed a really large fact table into a tablespace using data files from just that one volume group, then 248 disks would be sitting idle while just 8 were completely over-stressed. I've seen this more times than I care to admit, so watch out for it.

EXTENT MANAGEMENT

Another issue that seems to overly concern many DBAs is the issue of extent counts and sizing. Gone are the days of fitting objects into single extents. Yet I still see DBAs who want to keep their extent counts down—like it really matters. Let's see why it just doesn't fly anymore.

First, direct load operations are a must-have and are going to create an extent per parallel degree. So, a nightly data load with a parallel degree of 12 is going to create at least 4,380 extents over just one year (assuming that each parallel process needs only one extent for its portion of the overall data load). However, with real-world volumes in a typical data warehouse, it's not uncommon for that count to be 10–20 times that number, or 43,800–87,600 extents. Even if you use large extents, such as 2GB initial and next, the counts will still be very high. Remember that you may be loading tens of millions of records per night, and that is going to take more than just a few extents. So, your extent count over time is going to be high, period.

Second, data warehouses should be using locally managed tablespaces with uniform-sized extents. This type of tablespace management is far superior in terms of raw performance to that of dictionary-managed tablespaces. Moreover, it does not create any dictionary entries, which are often the actual concern of those DBAs obsessed with keeping the extent counts low. I've easily seen 15–20% improvements in data load and index creation times from using locally managed tablespaces. Furthermore, it seems to add about a 2–4% improvement across the board for all other operations as well, including queries (which I cannot easily explain). The real trick is to pick a uniform extent size that makes sense.

So how do you pick a good extent size? That's actually quite easy; just ask yourself how much disk space you're willing to waste each day. Remember our earlier nightly load example being done in parallel with degree 12? Assume the worst-case scenario: Each process will get one record that will not fit into the next to last extent, so each will create an extent that contains a single record. So, you get 12 extents that each contain a single record, which means that each is probably 95% or more unused. The next day's data load will create new extents and not use these partial extents since direct mode load means allocate new extents and then move the high-water mark. So how much waste can you tolerate? If you have 10MB extents and parallel degree 12, then you're going to potentially have 120MB waste each day. And while smaller means less waste, it does mean more extents.

I've found from 1–4 MB a good extent size when doing parallel. While it does create more extents, the waste is kept to a minimum and using parallel means that I can process lots of data. You'll have to find your own sweet spot.

UPDATES AND PATCHES

I've said several times throughout this book that data warehousing DBAs need to ride the bleeding edge of Oracle releases and patches. But, often the temptation exists to do things the OLTP way and wait six months before installing a new release or patch. I cannot stress how wrong this is. A successful data warehouse is going to depend heavily on key Oracle features. Queries need a star transformation explain plan, which needs hash joins, bitmap indexes, and statistics; data loads need parallel, direct mode inserts; and aggregates need either parallel, direct mode inserts or parallel, enabled "upserts" (i.e., the new MERGE command).

It's exactly these new features that have the most bugs, especially for large volumes of data and when using parallel operations. Table 9–1 is a selective sampling of about 1/20 of the Oracle 8.1.7.4 release notes. I've only included the sections that apply to data warehouses and the features they use most. Notice how many places the words "bitmap indexes" and "star transformations" appear. Also note how many times the phrases "wrong results" and "data or dictionary corruption" appear. All of a sudden, riding the bleeding edge does not sound so bad, does it?

Table 9–1   A Selective Sampling of the Oracle 8.1.7.4 Release Notes

Category	Fixed	BugNo	Description
Corruption			
	8174	1653112	EXCHANGE PARTITION does not check that FUNC-TIONAL index definitions match
	8174	2161512	INSERT /*+ APPEND*/ into table with FUNCTIONAL INDEX loads corrupt data
	8173	1616033	Direct load to composite partitioned table can corrupt local indexes
	8172	1360714	ALTER TABLE ADD PARTITION .. STORE IN with SUB-PARTITIONS can dump or corrupt dictionary
	8172	1527982	OERI:25012 / Bitmap index<->table mismatch after UPDATE of PARTITION KEY moves rows
Bitmap Indexes			
	8174	1916487	OERI:[QERBCROP KSIZE] possible from CREATE BIT-MAP INDEX on TO_DATE function
	8174	2156961	OERI:20040 possible from bitmap index
	8173	1346747	OERI:6101 / OERI:20063 possible using SERIALIZ-ABLE transactions with DML on BITMAP indexes
	8173	1358047	Wrong Results/Dump from Bitmap AND on BTREE range scan of concatenated index
	8173	1726833	OERI:13013 / Dump in kdudcp from UPDATE using range scan converted to BITMAPS
	8173	1751186	Wrong results / dump in qerixGetKey using bitmap indexes
	8173	1834495	OERI:12337 possible with many OR predicates on bit-map index prefix column
	8173	2065386	Mem. Corruption / OERI:KGHFRE2 / OERI:17172 pos-sible using bitmap indexes
	8173	2114246	Memory leak and long parse time for Part View with INLIST bitmap predicates
	8172	1380164	OERI:QKAGBY2 from aggregate GROUP BY with COUNT(*), Bitmap indexes and INLIST
Crash			
	8173	1711803	DBW & users may CRASH under heavy load on multi-CPU system with FAST_START_IO_TARGET set > 0
	8171	1482170	SMON may dump on cleanup of PARTITIONED INDEX ONLINE BUILD
Hangs/Spins			
	8174	2208570	ORA-4030 / ORA-4031 / spin during query optimization with STAR TRANSFORMATION and unmergable view

Table 9–1   A Selective Sampling of the Oracle 8.1.7.4 Release Notes (Continued)

Category	Fixed	BugNo	Description
	8173	1685119	OERI:KCBLIBR_USER_FOU / hang when interrupt (Ctrl-C) of PQ using STAR_TRANSFORMATION
	8173	1906596	PQ may hang when query involves ORDER BY, SUB-QUERY and UNION-ALL
	8172	1582923	A query may spin / dump with Row Level Security either STAR_TRANSFORMATION_ENABLED or _PUSH_JOIN_UNION_VIEW
Hash Join			
	8173	1839080	Memory leak possible using HASH join (ORA-4030)
Memory Corruption			
	8173	1711803	DBW & users may CRASH under heavy load on multi-CPU system with FAST_START_IO_TARGET set > 0
	8173	2002799	Wrong results / heap corruption from PQ with aggregates in inline view
	8173	2048336	OERI:150 / Memory corruption from interrupted STAR TRANSFORMATION
	8173	2065386	Mem. Corruption / OERI:KGHFRE2 / OERI:17172 possible using bitmap indexes
	8172	1732885	oeri:[KDIBR2R2R BITMAP] / memory corruption possible from BITMAP AND
Optimizer			
	8172	1582923	A query may spin / dump with Row Level Security either STAR_TRANSFORMATION_ENABLED or _PUSH_JOIN_UNION_VIEW
	8172	1587376	STAR_TRANSFORMATION_ENABLED=TRUE can cause INSERT as SELECT to dump
	8172	1620577	STAR_TRANSFORMATION_ENABLED=TRUE may dump in KKOSBPP or show poor performance
	8172	1715860	STAR_TRANSFORMATION_ENABLED = TRUE may give slow performance
	8171	1401235	ORA-900 from STAR_TRANSFORMATION_ENABLED with OR predicates to dimension table
	8171	1482423	OERI:4823 possible from STAR_TRANSFORMATION_ENABLED=TRUE
	8171	1490373	ORA-1008 can occur with STAR_TRANSFORMATION_ENABLED=true
Parallel Query (PQO)			
	8174	1548982	PQ Slaves do not use CURRENT_SCHEMA if set (ORA-12801/ORA-942 possible, or wrong table used)
	8174	1621835	Incorrect plan possible under parallel query

Table 9–1 A Selective Sampling of the Oracle 8.1.7.4 Release Notes (Continued)

Category	Fixed	BugNo	Description
	8174	1746797	Wrong results possible from PQ with SET operations in correlated subquery
	8174	1992414	ORA-12801 / ORA-932 possible from PQ referencing a colunn with a DESCENDING index
	8174	2091962	PQ against composite partitioned table with INLIST on subpartition key may error (OERI:QERPXMOBJVI5)
	8173	681179	Parallel TO_LOB(LONG) may dump
	8173	936107	OERI:15814 possible from parallel query
	8173	1020403	ORA-29900 possible from PQ using extensible ANCIL-LARY-PRIMARY operators
	8173	1183055	ORA-12801 / ORA-942 possible with PQ against synonym on another users view
	8173	1344653	ORA-7445[KOKLIGCURENV] possible running Text query in parallel
Partitioned Tables			
	8174	1653112	EXCHANGE PARTITION does not check that FUNCTIONAL index definitions match
	8174	1834530	OERI:25012 / wrong results after EXCHANGE PARTITION with indexes with different FREELIST /FREELIST GROUPS
	8174	2091962	PQ against composite partitioned table with INLIST on subpartition key may error (OERI:QERPXMOBJVI5)
	8174	2110573	ORA-439 attempting to IMPORT partitioned table into non-partitioned table without PARTIONING option
	8174	2121887	ORA-7445 [KKEHSL] possible with GLOBAL PARTITIONED INDEX and COLUMN HISTOGRAMS
	8174	2141535	ORA-604/ORA-942 possible from query against partitioned table
	8174	2157502	OERI:4819 possible when partition maintenence is running against an IOT
	8174	2162632	ORA-7445 from concurrent ANALYZE .. STATISTICS / CREATE INDEX against partitioned table
	8174	2199391	ADD/SPLIT [SUB]PARTITION can result in LOB partition in wrong tablespace
	8174	2201672	ORA-7445[MSQSEL] selecting from a view defined on other views with Partitioned tables
Performance			
	8174	2079526	"free buffer waits" / LRU latch contention possible on write intensive systems
	8171	1318267	INSERT AS SELECT may not share SQL when it should

Table 9–1   A Selective Sampling of the Oracle 8.1.7.4 Release Notes (Continued)

Category	Fixed	BugNo	Description
Query Rewrite (Including Materialized Views)			
	8174	1367842	Wrong results from query rewrite of SELECT COUNT(*) against MV with SELECT DISTINCT
	8174	1612352	ORA-30457 possible refreshing a nested materialized view
	8174	2097926	Dump possible from query using Function based index with MVIEW and QUERY_REWRITE_INTEGRITY=TRUSTED
	8174	2245289	ORA-12003 creating Materialized View with >32k SQL text
	8174	2263600	Query may not rewrite when expected
	8173	1314358	OERI:KKQSGCOL-1 possible on complex MV query
	8173	1618192	OERI:voprvl1 possible for INSERT into table SELECT FROM MATERIALIZED VIEW
	8173	1664189	Query rewrite does not occur if base table has a FUNCTIONAL index on it
	8173	1873265	SELECT COUNT(*) with QUERY_REWRITE and empty MV returns NULL instead of 0
	8173	1898834	Query rewrite may give incorrect results for outer joins
Resource Leaks (e.g., Memory Leaks)			
	8173	1782024	Memory leak in PQ slave during parallel propogation
	8173	1839080	Memory leak possible using HASH join (ORA-4030)
Space Management			
	8174	1937847	Space may be lost if migration of a tablespace to LOCALLY MANAGED is aborted
	8174	2209512	OERI:5325 possible during ALTER TABLE .. MOVE
	8172	1709816	OERI:[KTFBBSSEARCH-7] creating TABLE with FREELIST GROUPS in LOCALLY MANAGED AUTOALLOCATE tablespace
	8171	1499098	Direct loaded index blocks have fewer ITLs than possible for large INITRANS
Space Management— Bitmap Managed			
	8174	1642738	AUTOEXTEND of bitmap managed tablespaces does not try all files for space

Table 9–1   A Selective Sampling of the Oracle 8.1.7.4 Release Notes (Continued)

Category	Fixed	BugNo	Description
	8174	2157568	OERI:KCBGTCR_4 possible from query if segment in BITMAP tablespace is TRUNCATED
	8174	2194182	ORA-604 / ORA-1000 possible querying space information for BITMAPPED tablespace
Star Transformation			
	8174	1956846	ORA-7445[EVAOPN2] possible from STAR TRANSFORMATION if SUBQUERY_PRUNING enabled
	8174	2072348	OERI:[KKOJOCOL:2] from STAR TRANSFORMATION with duplicate table aliases
	8174	2144870	STAR TRANSFORMATION (FACT hint) may be ignored
	8174	2170565	Wrong results possible from STAR_TRANSFORMATION_ENABLED=TRUE temp table transformation
	8174	2172983	Wrong results / Dump from STAR_TRANSFORMATION of concatenated bitmap row source
	8174	2208570	ORA-4030 / ORA-4031 / spin during query optimization with STAR TRANSFORMATION and unmergable view
	8174	2241746	"FACT" hint may be ignored when valid - STAR TRANSFORMATION not used
	8174	2251373	Poor performance / CARTESIAN merge from TEMP TABLE STAR transformation
	8173	1461208	ORA-604 / ORA-918 possible from STAR TRANSFORMATION using views / subqueries
	8173	1565514	Wrong results/dump possible with STAR TRANSFORMATION and transitively generated predicate
Wrong Results			
	8174	1367842	Wrong results from query rewrite of SELECT COUNT(*) against MV with SELECT DISTINCT
	8174	2033324	Wrong results from BITMAP access of B*TREE index with all NULLABLE columns
	8174	2170565	Wrong results possible from STAR_TRANSFORMATION_ENABLED=TRUE temp table transformation
	8174	2228217	Join between partitioned and non-partitioned table may loose ORDER BY clause
	8173	1548495	Wrong results from PQ of partition-wise hash join on composite partitioned table
	8173	1565514	Wrong results/dump possible with STAR TRANSFORMATION and transitively generated predicate

Table 9–1   A Selective Sampling of the Oracle 8.1.7.4 Release Notes (Continued)

Category	Fixed	BugNo	Description
	8173	1587619	Wrong results possible from STAR TRANSFORMATION and SEMIJOIN
	8173	1759227	PQ may return wrong results selecting a COUNT(aggregate) column from a view
	8173	1793533	Wrong results possible from PQO with GROUP BY (affected by SORT_AREA_SIZE)
	8173	1855381	Wrong results possible from PQ partial piecewise join
Dumps/Abends			
	8174	2110054	Select COUNT(*) from a nested complex view with GROUP BY in inner view may dump in evaopn2
	8173	1787862	Dump possible from queries using ORDER BY clause
	8173	1805102	Dump possible from IN-LINE view "UNION" and "ORDER BY"
	8173	2004336	COUNT(NOT_NULL_COLUMN) may dump (QERIXGETKEY) if column referenced in WHERE clause
Errors/Internal Errors			
	8173	1478965	OERI:15160 possible with EXISTS/IN and HASH or MERGE ALWAYS_SEMI_JOIN
	8173	1748384	OERI:qksopOptASJLf1 / dump in kkeajsel with ALWAYS_SEMI_JOIN=MERGE/HASH with SUBQUERY containing OR of correlated variable
	8172	1397075	OERI:KCBGCUR_9 from SMON during temp seg cleanup for segment in read only LOCALLY MANAGED TABLESPACE
	8172	1656588	ORA-1008 from STAR_TRANSFORMATION_ENABLED and TRUNC()
	8171	962560	ORA-25128 possible for INSERT .. SELECT from table with "DISABLE VALIDATE" constraint
	8171	1500717	ORA-903 with STAR_TRANSFORMATION and non alphanumeric table name
	8171	1533922	OERI:KGLCHK2_1 possible referencing a SEQUENCE with STAR_TRANSFORMATION or PARTITION_VIEW_ENABLED or _PUSH_JOIN_UNION_VIEW

Index

A

Ad-hoc queries
  bitmap indexes, 92–95, 102–7
  cost-based optimizer, 108
  dimension tables, 86
  fact tables, 86
  first-generation star schema query
    optimization, 88–89
  fourth-generation star schema query
    optimization, 93–95
  initialization parameters, 99–102
  overview, 85–86
  second-generation star schema query
    optimization, 89–90
  star optimization evolution, 87–95
  star schema index design, 102–7
  star transformation, 96–99, 109–11
  statistics collection method, 108
  third-generation star schema query
    optimization, 90–92, 95
  tuning requirements, 86–87
Aggregates
  deciding what to build, 148–50
  as distinct phase in overall process, 154–63
  end-user needs and, 149
  inserts, 156–59
  loading architecture, 150–53
  materialized views, 163–68
  overview, 147–48
  scenarios for, 156–63
  size of, 149–50
  upserts and Oracle 8i, 159–62
  upserts and Oracle 9i, 162–63
Architecture, loading, 121–22

B

Backup and recovery, 190–92
Benchmarks, 186–87
Bitmap indexes, 92–95, 102–7, 199
Business intelligence options, 15–17

C

Challenges of data warehouse, 12
Clustering, 47–49
Common parallel hardware architectures, 45–51
Complex partitions
  in Oracle 8i, 179–83
  in Oracle 9i, 183–86
  overview, 173–74
Cooked files, 62–63
Corruption, 199
Cost-based optimizer, 108
CPU usage, 35–39, 43–51
Crash, 199

D

Database application
  categorizations, 3
  characteristics, 5–6
  development life cycle, 10–11
Data warehouse
  application development lifecycle, 11–12
  challenges of, 12
  EIS compared, 9–10
  large database compared, 4–6
  loading. See loading data warehouse
  overview, 1–4
"Data Warehouse Performance Enhancements
    with Oracle 9i" (white paper), 84
Deploying loading architecture, 145
Design options for partitions, 170–71
Dimensional hierarchies, 76–78
Dimension tables, 71–73, 86
Disk arrays, 53–57
Disk configuration, 52–57
Disk space, 52–57
Dumps/abends, 204

E

End-user needs and aggregates, 149
Errors/internal errors, 204

inform**IT**

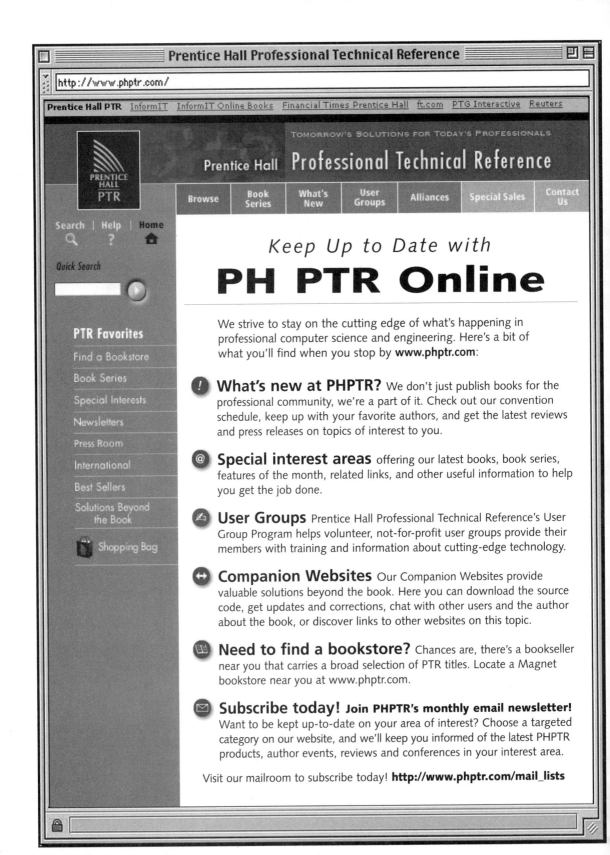

Prentice Hall Professional Technical Reference

http://www.phptr.com/

Prentice Hall PTR   InformIT   InformIT Online Books   Financial Times Prentice Hall   ft.com   PTG Interactive   Reuters

TOMORROW'S SOLUTIONS FOR TODAY'S PROFESSIONALS

Prentice Hall **Professional Technical Reference**

| Browse | Book Series | What's New | User Groups | Alliances | Special Sales | Contact Us |

Search | Help | Home

Quick Search

PTR Favorites

Find a Bookstore

Book Series

Special Interests

Newsletters

Press Room

International

Best Sellers

Solutions Beyond the Book

Shopping Bag

Keep Up to Date with
PH PTR Online

We strive to stay on the cutting edge of what's happening in professional computer science and engineering. Here's a bit of what you'll find when you stop by **www.phptr.com**:

What's new at PHPTR? We don't just publish books for the professional community, we're a part of it. Check out our convention schedule, keep up with your favorite authors, and get the latest reviews and press releases on topics of interest to you.

Special interest areas offering our latest books, book series, features of the month, related links, and other useful information to help you get the job done.

User Groups Prentice Hall Professional Technical Reference's User Group Program helps volunteer, not-for-profit user groups provide their members with training and information about cutting-edge technology.

Companion Websites Our Companion Websites provide valuable solutions beyond the book. Here you can download the source code, get updates and corrections, chat with other users and the author about the book, or discover links to other websites on this topic.

Need to find a bookstore? Chances are, there's a bookseller near you that carries a broad selection of PTR titles. Locate a Magnet bookstore near you at www.phptr.com.

Subscribe today! Join PHPTR's monthly email newsletter! Want to be kept up-to-date on your area of interest? Choose a targeted category on our website, and we'll keep you informed of the latest PHPTR products, author events, reviews and conferences in your interest area.

Visit our mailroom to subscribe today! **http://www.phptr.com/mail_lists**